MARGARET JOHN JANKOWSKI

# COMMON THREADS

Delivering hope and meaning
through sewing machines

LITTLE CREEK PRESS®
AND BOOK DESIGN
MINERAL POINT, WISCONSIN

Little Creek Press
5341 Sunny Ridge Road
Mineral Point, WI 53565

ORDERING INFORMATION **Quantity sales.** Special discounts are available on quantity purchases by corporations, associations, and others. For details, contact info@littlecreekpress.com

**Orders by US trade bookstores and wholesalers.**
Please contact Little Creek Press or Ingram for details.

Printed in the United States of America

Cataloging-in-Publication Data
Names: Jankowski, Margaret John, author
Title: Common Threads. Description: Mineral Point, WI. Little Creek Press, 2023
Identifiers: LCCN: 2023906817 | ISBN: 978-1-955656-53-5
Subjects: Biography and Autobiography—Women

Cover art: Carl Landgren
Book design by Mimi Bark and Little Creek Press

To Walter
who believed that nothing
is impossible.

"A visionary is defined as both a dreamer and as someone with foresight and imagination. Margaret Jankowski had a vision of helping others, saw how it could be achieved, and then engaged the collective power and generosity of others to bring her idea to fruition. Through her faith, compassion, and sheer willpower, Margaret has positively impacted thousands of lives, and like a pebble thrown in a pond, the ripples continue to spread outward in ever-increasing circles. My heart nearly burst at this tangible manifestation of how one person can make such an incredible difference."

-ALEX ANDERSON, founding partner of
The Quilt Show and *The Quilt Life* magazine

"I can't begin to express how much our organization appreciated partnering with Margaret and The Sewing Machine Project for sewing machine donations following the devastating losses due to Hurricane Katrina in 2005. The continuous shipment of sewing machines to the cultural community provided hope and stability to artists in the various African-based art forms of music, masquerade, and processional celebrations. Because of The SMP's generous efforts to the cultural community, many artists were able to recover and are again sharing their beautiful creations in exhibitions around the world."

-HERREAST J. HARRISON, the Guardians Institute/
Donald Harrison Sr. Cultural Museum

"Imbued with grace notes of hope and humility, Margaret Jankowski's *Common Threads* reveals how one compassionate woman's determination to help others inspired the Sewing Machine Project, a remarkable nonprofit dedicated to empowering people in need with the gift of a sewing machine. Quilters and sewing enthusiasts in particular will be moved by this compelling story of how kindness and generosity can transform lives and strengthen communities."

-JENNIFER CHIAVERINI, *New York Times* bestselling
author of the Elm Creek Quilts novels

"I am delighted that Margaret has written down the story (to date) of The Sewing Machine Project, as I have watched it unfold over many years. What began as one person's compassionate response to suffering has become an ongoing act of faith by many. But at its core is Margaret's trust in the goodness of humanity. The SMP has grown not so much because of a grand plan but through an openness to Spirit by Margaret and a growing community of others with her. It is a story worth documenting and sharing widely as it offers a powerful example of what individuals and small groups can do to make a difference in a world that holds such great need and suffering."

—REVEREND WINTON BOYD, Center for Courage and Renewal, United Church of Christ

"Margaret Jankowski takes us on a journey that starts with a simple, altruistic idea—the notion that a functioning sewing machine can make a difference in a person's (usually a woman's) life. Since 2005, The Sewing Machine Project has distributed over 4,000 sewing machines to people who need them. Sewers are among the kindest, most generous folks on earth, and it is no wonder that this idea resonates. If you would like proof that one person, one idea, can generate meaningful change, read this wonderful book!"

—MARIANNE FONS, co-creator of Fons & Porter's Love of Quilting on public television stations nationwide

"The Sewing Machine Project is an amazing ministry of faith. Margaret Jankowski recognized how access to a simple sewing machine could enrich and enhance the lives of women in the U.S. and around the world. She has poured her heart and soul into finding ways to connect communities with the resources they need to be able to start their own sewing ministry. Lives are changed!"

—PASTOR JULIA HOLLISTER, First Congregational Church

# Prologue

"Whatever you can do or dream you can, begin it.
Boldness has genius, power, and magic in it."

-JOHANN WOLFGANG VON GOETHE

What is an idea? A spark? A push? A breath? What prompts us to pick up one idea from the hundreds that flit through our minds each day? How do we tune our spirit such that it discerns the voice of the Divine in an idea we see as ours alone? And when do we say *yes*?

This is the story of an idea, the organization the idea inspired, and the deep lessons within. Presented in snapshots, tiny windows into the idea's growth, this frame-by-frame narrative is the only way I can think of to present it, for this is how it has been revealed to me. The idea's profound insistence on carving its own course is undeniable.

Dear new owner of this machine,

I got this sewing machine in 1957 and I had many happy hours of sewing on it. I hope you love it as much as I did.

Happy Sewing from me to thee.

The idea found me.

# Chapter 1

"There are two ways to live your life—one as if nothing
is a miracle, the other as if everything is a miracle."

-ALBERT EINSTEIN

The idea found me.

Arriving on an icy February morning, the idea landed like a whisper,
like a door ajar, inviting me in. Had I been able to push the door
open and squint into the future, I'd surely have stepped back and
pulled the door shut, not believing it possible or myself capable of
such an endeavor. But as it was, a ray of light was all there was, and
that was enough.

The idea pulled me closer. It captured me.

I leaned back and stared through the window, my tired office chair
offering a *creak* as I pulled a worn blanket around my shoulders. I
inhaled the comfortably familiar scents of my children and our little
dog, smells that were "home" to me. Winter howled through the

cracks and crevices of our drafty, hundred-year-old farmhouse. A distorted view of the world met my gaze through the wavy window glass—swirling snow, skeletal trees, the icy gray of Lake Monona. Chill crept in through cracks in caulk and floorboards—through the walls themselves. I pulled my blanket closer.

Returning my eyes to the computer screen, I savored my Saturday morning quiet time. With kids and husband quietly absorbed in their own interests, I caught up on emails and happily settled into exploring the *Threads* magazine website, filling my mind with textiles and techniques, the accouterments of sewing. I love to sew, and dipping into news of the sewing world with new projects, colors, and ideas transported me.

Then, it happened. Had the idea been there for a while, hovering in the high corners of the house, waiting for me to slow down so it could show itself?

The article appeared on the left column of the page—no special font, no flashing lights, and yet it caught my attention—an idea waiting to be birthed.

"Come here. Look at this," it whispered.

Written by Frances Harrison, a BBC reporter in Sri Lanka, the article's story sang with loss and promise. Traveling with three women back to their village after the December 2004 tsunami, Ms. Harrison interviewed each about her life before and after the storm. Carefully stepping through the rubble of dirt and rocks—the remains of the road—the women picked a new path home, with no idea of what "home" meant anymore. Gently, Ms. Harrison asked, "What do you hope to find?" One by one, they offered short inventories of the practical and the precious, remains of life's belongings, tossed helter-skelter as the water swept the land.

It was Vahashani's turn:

*"I just hope I find my sewing machine."*

Vahashani went on, detailing how she saved for the machine, her joy and sense of accomplishment in the purchase, and the importance of this tool to her family. She sketched her dream of teaching her daughter to sew, hoping that this skill could bring joy and an income, something Vahashani had struggled to achieve.

I read the article one, two, three times. The idea stopped hovering, then settled on my keyboard as I said *yes,* noting neither the agreement nor the fledgling idea lodging in my heart.

Tom Waits once said, ". . . songs are strange, they're very simple, they come quickly. If you don't take them, they'll move on. They'll go to somebody else. Someone else will write it down." I'm pretty sure ideas are like songs—hovering near us, around us—gifts of a mystery beyond our sight. We say *yes* or we say *no,* often without knowing, rarely understanding the scope of what might be asked of us. With my *yes,* a door swung open, beckoning me further. A path I couldn't yet see appeared before me, and I took the first step.

I worked part time at Hans' Sewing Center, a sewing machine dealership in Madison, Wisconsin, selling sewing machines and teaching people how to use them. The job fit well with my main occupation as a stay-at-home mom. I had worked several part-time jobs over the years, each offering a small supplement to our income and much-needed time with adults. Diverse and seemingly disconnected, I often wondered how the experience gained in each part-time position could possibly knit together into anything the working world would value once my children were grown and on their own. I had served as the administrator for my children's nursery school, writing grants and managing accreditation processes. I'd sewn outerwear for a design studio, learning how to manipulate powerful industrial sewing machines. I was a substitute teacher in our local school district.

When I answered an ad searching for a sewing teacher and sales-person at Hans', I discovered a welcoming and creative workspace. A hive of color and creativity, the shop offered an opportunity to share sewing with like-minded makers while contributing to the family coffers. Hans' staff and customers were like family to me. Dave, the owner, had grown up in the business, and Hans was his father. Maintaining a tradition of Swiss precision, Dave focused mainly on the technical aspects of the machines, while we, the sales staff, dove into the more personal side of sewing. Each sale began with a conversation designed to get acquainted with the customer.

"Tell me about the kind of sewing you do," I'd say. "Do you quilt? Then maybe a machine with a larger throat would work well for you." Or, "Are you primarily a garment sewer? I find this machine to be especially nimble when stitching the subtle curves of a blouse."

Beyond the practical, as a sewer, I understand the less tangible aspects of sewing. I know the magic of the creative process, the way the world opens when planning a project in three dimensions. I delight in the way fabric glides through the fingers and over the cool metal machine bed. The sales discussion also included the customer's budget, but the features and personalities of the machines sang the loudest. This brought light to the customer's eyes as she imagined all she could do with a new machine. I helped to paint that picture.

Often, customers would reflect on what their current machine meant to them. Usually, it was characterized as a trusted friend (although occasionally a formidable enemy!), attesting to the joined history of sewer and machine. Some machines had previous chapters. "My machine was my mother's, my grandmother's." Sometimes there was a plan for its future. "I'll give it to my daughter."

But often, I'd hear, "I wonder what I will do with my old machine."

As I read and reread the article, the imbalance between Vahashani's loss and my customers' abundance presented itself in stark relief. It seemed so simple—I'll just collect machines in Wisconsin and send them to Sri Lanka. I would ask Dave if I could have some of the used machines.

The door had opened enough to beckon without frightening me away. I still didn't know who would receive the machines, how I would get them there, where they would go, or how I would pay for shipping, but there was no doubt within me. I had already said yes.

Different makes and models of machines are like old friends–difficult to part with and somehow familiar to those who receive them.

# Chapter 2

*In my dream, fog hugs me like a shroud, like a birthing blanket. The trail I walk is narrow, allowing only one foot set carefully in front of the other. I can see where my foot will land on the worn path, but no more. In the thick fog, I can sense, rather than see, the pines around me and the path in front of me. The air is still, and the world unearthly quiet. I am completely calm—a reflection of the peace that lives within and surrounds me. I feel no fear as I set my foot forward, pausing mid-step to absorb the stillness.*

I awoke gently with the dream and its accompanying sense of calm still floating in my head. Lingering in the space between dreaming and waking, my breath deep and measured, the dream's narrow path haunted me. Some call them *desire lines*—paths made by feet finding a new way where there was no prior path. Perhaps my dreamed path was a *desire line* of sorts—one I was meant to follow.

The windows rattled with the March wind as the blue light of morning revealed the dancing silhouettes of bare branches. It was Saturday, and I was scheduled to work, but this was not just any work day. Before my feet even hit the floor, my head was in planning mode, to-do lists pinned in the front of my mind.

Only hours later, I was busily tidying the front tables at Hans' Sewing Center. The tables formed a makeshift classroom, a space I knew well. The big windows welcomed natural light. Simultaneously exposed and contained, the space exuded a steady sense of purpose and focus. This is where people learned to use their new sewing machines, to quilt in free motion, to build clothing that fit. Hans' was a creative oasis with desire lines invisibly embedded in the worn carpet, trails left by eager sewers, hungry for inspiration.

Raising my eyes to check the time, I looked through the front window. Faces greeted me, smiling back. A line had formed along the sidewalk to the front door steps. Cradling sewing machines and hefting shopping bags, people waited, and I knew they were waiting for me.

I'd been talking to my friend Bob only weeks before, sharing my heady dream of sewing machines and waiting recipients far away. Bob was the general manager of one of our local television stations and suggested I make my pitch on television.

"You'll get more machines that way," Bob said. "I can help you."

Within days, I was in the hot seat, being interviewed on the local news, sketching out an idea only beginning to take shape. My nerves hummed. I wasn't used to being in the spotlight. Holding up a piece of printer paper with a hand drawing of a wave, reading, "Tsunami Relief," my voice quavered as I announced a collection day in March, a Saturday morning when people could drop off sewing machines and supplies at the store. Would anyone hear me? Would anyone come?

Bob's wife, Pam, gave me a call. "Do you actually know anyone in Sri Lanka?" she asked. "Who will you ship these machines to?"

The questions swirled in an unfolding interior dialogue. If I found machines, where would I send them? What address would go on the boxes?

"I work with a man named Bahee," Pam went on. "He's quite active in the Madison chapter of the American Hindu Association. He may be able to help." I contacted Bahee and learned their group was working with orphanages overflowing with children after the storm.

"I know they would love some machines," he said. As an established nonprofit, the Hindu Association could share donation receipts with me that I could give to anyone who donated a machine.

I unlocked the front door. The Swiss cowbell hanging from the security chain clanged. One by one, people entered the store with their offerings, smiling and shaking off the cold. Their measured steps and posture belied the weight of their packages—sewing machines and bags filled to overflowing with bright printed fabric.

"This was my grandma's," offered the first woman in line as I helped her lift the machine to the table. I lifted the cover to unveil a smoky blue Dressmaker machine. "Grandma was an excellent seamstress," she added.

I ran my hands over the machine's curves, imagining her grandma's hands doing the same. In its day, this machine would have been a prize to any seamstress.

"Grandma was always at this machine," the woman continued. "She made all of the clothes in the house. She even made Grandpa's suits!"

The next man hefted a black garbage bag filled with fabric, pushing it closer to the table and opening it.

"My wife asked me to bring this. She has tons of fabric." He rolled the plastic bag down to reveal the treasure, carefully folded cottons catching the light.

"Wow, these are beautiful!" I whispered.

"She spent all last night sorting and washing these, then packing them for you. My wife loves to sew. She was excited to be able to help someone else enjoy something she loves so much." I pulled out a stack of soft folded calico, my "thank you" escaping like breath.

The line outside gradually transformed into a crowd inside as people nudged their way through the door, escaping the cold. I scanned their faces, searching for impatience but finding none. A community was forming. People chatted with one another, making small talk about where they lived and what they carried. Some shared details about the machines they held—who it had belonged to, what it had created—chapters in the life of a sewing machine.

One by one, people approached the table. Unlocking stiff clasps or lifting a plastic cover, givers unveiled sewing machines of all shapes and sizes, ages, makes and models. My nostrils tickled with the smells of oil and brushed metal, rust and age, or a dank cloud of mildew. My right hand gently rolled the hand wheel, feeling for movement and play, while my left hand cupped the machine's needle bar housing as I eyed the take-up lever's rise and fall. I listened carefully for catching, for missed notes that would call for later evaluation. I accepted them all, one by one, a part of a new community of tools with chapters yet to be revealed. Color, loud and soft, popped out of the fabric-crammed shopping bags and cardboard boxes as they accumulated at my feet, cushioning the metal of the machines.

The morning flew by, a steady stream of givers offering what they had, joyful in the giving, tearful in the memories, grateful to know their machine's story would continue. The store closed at noon on Saturdays, and the sea of people gradually subsided. I walked the final donor to the door, thanking him and saying goodbye, then turned to survey the morning's wealth, filling the entire front half of the store. We had collected at least fifty machines.

And I had worried that no one would come.

My coworkers, responsible for running the store during the morning's flurry, waded through the pool of bags, boxes, and machines and joined me at the front of the store to begin sorting and then carrying weighty, black garbage bags to the back warehouse; unwieldy cardboard boxes pushed and shuffled across the carpeting to join the bags; sewing machines lined up beneath the front windows. Checking their watches, Julie and Sandra said their goodbyes, eager to move on with their weekends. The Swiss cowbell signaled their departure, and the fading echo gradually stilled to silence. I stood in the quiet.

The unfolding was real—the line of machines, visible evidence. Infused with excitement and peace, I lifted a machine to the table, lifting the cover and untangling the cord. I plugged it in and pressed the foot control. The whir of the machine was music.

Machines were welcome tools when they arrived at orphanages in India and Sri Lanka and were put into service at once.

# Chapter 3

Black as the night sky, smaller than most but surprisingly heavy, the Singer 99K is a solid, basic sewing machine. I gently lowered the machine into its snug nest. The 99K only goes forward and backward but marches in a precisely measured stitch. As machines go, it is perfect.

Bahee and I stood at the table, surveying the goods ready to be packed. In the spirit of collaboration, we combined our shipments—the necessary medical supplies (bandages, syringes, tubing) and one sewing machine per box. Clean cottons and comforting stuffed toys were nestled around each machine, soft against the metal frame. Every box carried a slightly different offering. We packed five at a time, talking while we worked. Bahee provided a lens through which I could catch a glimpse of lives so different from my own. With his words, he painted pictures of Sri Lanka and India, places I'd never visited. Through his eyes, I could see the land and its people—the children finding a new path in the orphanages and the adults around them trying to make this new, parentless world somehow okay.

Bahee and I began by taking a test box to the post office to be weighed so we could estimate the cost of one package's journey. Including the shipping and a power transformer, each box would cost about $75 to ship. Neither the Hindu Association, stretched already with purchasing relief supplies, nor my bank account could cover the expense of sending several boxes. I had no idea where or how I would come up with funding, yet the words slipped over my lips. "We'll find the money."

And the money came. My friend Leslie, a Girl Scout troop leader, called, saying, "I told our local council about the sewing machine idea. The girls do an annual fundraiser called 'Thinking Day,' and this year, they would like you to receive the proceeds." Weeks later, a check for $500 arrived.

People I knew and people I'd never met sent money. I didn't remember having asked anyone, yet somehow I had asked and been answered. Notes of encouragement accompanied many of the checks—little nudges and nods that moved me forward. Every few weeks, I would carefully open the brown envelope where the money was kept and count its contents.

It was April 2005. Budding leaves brightened the branches that brushed the window. The world was soft and green with spring. Every sewing machine needed to be checked. Like the idea itself, the supporting structure grew within me. Every sewing machine needed to work perfectly before being included in a shipment. I knew that the people who would receive the machines had many struggles in their lives, and I didn't want to add one more. I wanted these machines to be a gift, plain and simple, not an added headache. My coworkers, generous with their time, gave up Sunday mornings to sit at the table with me, looking over each machine. Carefully threading and oiling, we checked for movement, and the air filled with the whir of motors. We tested each machine's stitches and functions, ensuring each one was nothing short of excellent.

We evaluated one machine after another, marveling at their differences and similarities. While we worked, we shared what was on our hearts. Sewing does that, creating a magic that opens us. While hands are busy, words dance.

"Oh, look at this one!" Eileen exclaimed, lifting the lid on an aged pink beauty. We all paused to admire it.

"Look at this perfect stitch!" Rebecca said.

Every week, we would meet to check machines, the lineup growing as more machines arrived in the weeks following the initial collection. After evaluating and adjusting them, we had seventy-five working sewing machines gleaming and ready to travel.

I sat at the desk in my home office, eyeing the welcome spring outside, holding the brown envelope. I had done the math. Gently pulling the pile of cash and checks from their brown cocoon, I sorted and added the donations, making notes on a rudimentary balance sheet. I still needed an additional $2,000 to purchase power supplies and ship all seventy-five machines. I'd felt so confident that I could gather this money. But could I? I said a silent prayer. *Please shine a light on the best way to find this money.* I leaned back with a sigh, my eyes returning to the fresh green outside the window.

The back door pushed open, and a rush of spring poured into the house as my daughter, Maddie, arrived home from middle school. At thirteen, she kept her interactions with me brief. My son, Alec, a freshman, was caught up in the newness of high school. Maddie shrugged off her backpack.

"Hi, Mom," she said.

"Hi, honey! How was school?"

"Fine. We're going on a field trip tomorrow. Oh—and the student council is collecting money for the tsunami. I need to take some money tomorrow."

She pounded up the steps to her room, closing the door behind her. Strains of Green Day seeped under the door and down the stairs. Teen drama hung in the air.

"Tsunami relief," I mused as I sat back in my chair. "I wonder . . ."

I picked up the phone and dialed the school district office. Bev, the secretary, answered. "Hi, Bev, how are you? Maddie says there is a tsunami fundraiser going on?"

"Yes," replied Bev. "All of the schools in the district are involved. The Student Council has organized it."

"Where will the money be sent?"

"We haven't decided yet."

"Well, let me tell you what I have going on," and I began painting a picture—the machines ready and waiting and the children in the orphanages who could benefit so much from these tools.

"We still need money to make the project work," I added without revealing the price tag. "Just think of how meaningful it would be for our kids if they knew they were helping other kids!"

Bev's voice held a smile. "Well, you know that everything in the district is a process. But we do have a meeting this week, and the fundraiser is on the agenda. I'll tell people about your idea."

I thanked Bev and hung up, heading outside for a break. Sitting on the front steps, I inhaled deeply as spring air vibrated with new growth and hope. I had asked out loud this time and now needed to let the idea simmer and grow.

At the end of the week, Bev called. "The meeting went well. The group voted to give you everything that is collected. It'll be another week or so before we have a total." I thanked her, my mind humming with numbers, and said a silent prayer.

Another week and a half passed, and the anticipation of Bev's call beat in me like an erratic heartbeat. When the phone rang, and I heard Bev's voice on the other end, I held my breath and listened as she described the fundraiser's wrap-up.

"The kids raised $2,015! Can you believe it?" Bev said. "We'll be sending you the check. Who should I make it out to?"

Bev's words continued as I hung on the number—$2,015.

"Thank you, Bev," I said, pulling myself back into the moment. "Thank you so much."

Hanging up, I sat in quiet gratitude, marveling at the outcome. I'd simply asked for guidance without naming how I thought the solution would look.

Bahee and I prepared another five boxes for travel. Sinking a solid beige JC Penney machine into the fifth carton, I admired how the face of each sewing machine reflected its era and expectations, dreams, and consumer demands. Shapes and colors changed with the fashion of the times. Tight angles gave way to curves. Industrial-looking brown metal bodies gave way to pinks, blues, and greens. In the 1970s, there were groovy flowered sewing machines that looked something like Scooby Doo's Mystery Machine. I loved imagining the era and the marketing around each model. Returning from my distraction, I carefully tucked a roll of floral cotton, white splashed with happy orange flowers and tiny green leaves, into the box, rocking it for balance. The soft fabric cushioned and protected the machine's edges and provided stability and a happy splash of color. I nudged the transformer in beside the machine.

Bahee was eager to get our shipment to the post office. People in Sri Lanka were waiting. I tried to imagine the setting, the room where the boxes would land, be received and opened. A smile spread through me as I tucked in a few more soft toys. "I hope they love this," I said to Bahee.

He paused, one hand still inside the box he was packing, and looked at me, his face radiant. "You have no idea what a gift this is," he said.

Brought together with a simple wish to help, Bahee and I maintained a businesslike relationship. We created sets of five boxes, each a treasure chest of necessities with a few soft toys thrown in— something the children in the orphanages would instantly understand.

After each shipment, we waited for confirmation that our cargo had landed. Photos arrived of the unpacking at the other end. We saw sari-clad women cradling the familiar machines and small groups of barefoot children smiling shyly. The pictures helped bring this distant world closer. I stared at my computer screen, scrolling through the photos—one, then the next. The immensity of the distance and the tsunami's destructive path, the orphans' cries, and their caretakers' mighty responsibility were all captured in low-resolution colored images.

Once a set of boxes had landed, Bahee and I began planning for the next shipment. I gathered five readied machines and prepared them for their journey. Then Bahee and I would meet and stand together, carefully packing five boxes. I walked this path, hardly knowing I was walking it, not knowing how far it extended, just taking one small step at a time. No matter when it ended, I would know I had helped a few people, and that would be enough. But then the next step would beckon, and I followed, a compass deep within me pointing the way.

Tell me, how does one NOT fall in love with New Orleans?

# Chapter 4

L ate July in New Orleans is hotter than a hushpuppy straight from the fryer. I stepped out of the Sheraton Hotel onto bustling Canal Street. Having lived briefly in the South, I'd learned you don't move fast in this heat. You saunter. You sashay. But you definitely don't run. Sweat beaded on my forehead.

When my boss, Dave, asked who would like to attend the Janome sewing machine conference in New Orleans, I eagerly stepped forward. Like those offered by every sewing machine brand, the annual conference was candy to a sewer. New machines were introduced in hands-on workshops, allowing participants to fall in love with the latest technology and its creativity. I jumped at the chance, gathered my sewing supplies, and planned my conference schedule.

Before leaving, I visited the readied machines waiting in the back warehouse and spoke to them assuredly. "I'll be back in a week!" I said before closing the door.

Stepping into the bustling world where one is expected to network was daunting. I preferred the quiet of my sewing room. Doing my best to quiet my nerves, I vowed to push myself.

I gathered my suitcase from the spinning luggage belt at the New Orleans airport and headed for the shuttle line. Two men in matching shirts queued in front of me, and I noted the sewing machine company name embroidered on their pockets.

"Do you work for Janome?" I asked (quietly patting myself on the back for speaking up).

"Yep, we're sales managers. I'm Dave, from London, Ontario. And this is Jim from Toronto."

"I'm from a Janome dealership," I offered. "Looks like we're attending the same conference."

We rode together through the city as the shuttle deposited travelers at several hotels. As Jim and Dave prepared to step off at the Sheraton, I pushed myself again.

"Hey, I'm on my own. If your group is doing something fun, could I tag along?"

Dave handed me his business card. "You bet!" he said. "Let's meet at the opening ceremony and make plans from there."

I settled back into my seat, proud of myself. This tiny bit of networking might seem minor to some, but it felt like a success to me.

I'd visited New Orleans only once before, in seventh grade, with my parents, riding the City of New Orleans train route straight south, Chicago to Memphis, on to Jackson, and into New Orleans. My memories were a noisy blur of beignets, jazz, and Mardi Gras beads. I stepped out of the shuttle bus at my hotel and looked around at the buildings and the streets. Nothing looked familiar three decades later.

That evening, I gathered myself for the opening, fighting the urge to forego the crowd and find a quiet dinner on my own. I took one last look in the mirror and headed out, walking the two blocks to the Sheraton, where the conference took place. I smiled at the others on the elevator, a single among groups of twos and threes and fours, all ready for a party. I put on my best convivial face.

Stepping off the elevator, I spotted Dave standing with a big group. I wandered closer, hoping he would spot me. He turned. "Margaret! Here she is. Come and meet everyone." And just like that, I was absorbed into a group of kind, warm Canadians. My nerves quieted as I picked up a glass of wine and became part of the crowd. Later that evening, we walked together, talking and laughing, through the French Quarter as if we'd known each other forever. I smiled, grateful I had pushed myself beyond my edge.

Conference days were filled with lessons on the newest sewing machines. Learning how to sell these mechanical triumphs is best accomplished through learning how to use them and falling in love with their features. Selling is easy when you love and believe in what you're selling. The hotel's meeting rooms came alive with quilting techniques, sewing classes, machines, and enthusiasm.

During scheduled breaks, most attendees followed the call of coffee in the lobby or lunch nearby, but a different siren song sang in my ears. I headed out into the heat. A walk down Canal Street took me past electronics and souvenir shops, a guy with a sign begging for beer money, and girly show posters. I turned left, diving into the French Quarter.

The narrow streets quickly became familiar relatives—saucy Uncle Bourbon Street and refined Auntie Royal Street. Chartres Street, with its weird assemblage of shops, was that aunt with whom I'd never quite found a connection, and Decatur seemed like that wild cousin to whom I was attracted and, at the same time, a bit afraid.

With sidewalks jutting up and down, gaping holes ready to twist an ankle, I was careful to watch my step, though it wasn't easy—my eyes were drawn in every direction. I paused to snap a picture of ferns gracefully poking through a balcony's ironwork and then stepped back to peer into a shop window. I let a street musician's music fill me and admired an artist's painting jauntily hung on a fence. New Orleans was like a conductor directing me in a new rhythm, and the instrument of my body could not resist response.

Each evening, I would find the Canadians, and they would gather me in. Heading off into the noise and life of the city, we explored the French Quarter and Frenchman Street, infused with the bawdiness of the city, emboldened by one another. We hit clubs and lounges, voodoo shops, and ghost tours while getting to know one another better. As days passed, I measured the distance from where I'd been when I first got off the plane to where I arrived with each encounter.

When the time came to fly home, I felt tight threads connecting me to this curious city, a bit of New Orleans lodging within me like a souvenir. I said goodbye to my new friends and watched as the crescent swirl of the river became a tiny spot below the plane. I felt as though I'd left a bit of my spirit behind, loosely dancing through the streets. Talk about the ghosts that haunt the alleys and buildings of New Orleans is common—ship captains and despondent widows, voodoo queens and vampires. I think they are joined by bits of spirit left behind by people like me who fall in love with this place and choose to linger.

Back in Madison, I resumed my job, adding to it the training of the rest of our staff and sharing what I had learned. I generated anticipation about the new machines by sharing photos and describing emerging technology. Filled with the energy of new ideas, infused with the city's pulse, I easily conveyed the conference's excitement. In small groups, I passed around the samples I had made in workshops, describing the new techniques I had learned. Dave and I poured over machine specs and price lists, filling out order forms.

Gradually I returned to collecting machines and preparing of our next Sri Lanka shipment. Standing in the shadowy warehouse space behind the store, I checked on the remaining fifty machines awaiting deployment. The single bulb dangling from the warehouse's high ceiling offered strands of light, illuminating enough of the high wooden shelves to count the machines without revealing their details. Sliding a machine forward into the light, I ran my hands over her curves, marveling at the kindness and mystery that landed it here. I jotted a mental note to get in touch with Bahee to put our next packing date on the calendar. Little by little, I settled back into the familiar pace of home and work, the memory of New Orleans, an exotic spice among my salt and pepper days.

When a storm began to build off the Gulf Coast later in August, I paid keen attention. Images on the news, a cloudy spiral, looked ominous. "This is going to be a big one," meteorologists warned. Evacuation orders were issued in regions threatened by the storm's broad path. Folks in New Orleans had heard this sort of thing before. Many people left, but many stayed. Those who chose to stay busily stocked up on water, food, and generators, as they were no strangers to turbulent weather. Windows were boarded. The highway was rerouted in one direction, and a river of cars flowed out of the city. As the storm grew and gathered force, panic rose. A city known for its easy, relaxed attitude became frantic. People charged the exits.

The nation held its breath as Hurricane Katrina made landfall on August 29, 2005. Katrina was a perfect storm, a quilt of disaster woven of a city below sea level, deteriorating infrastructure, a deficient levee system, and poverty. Katrina shook that quilt wide, and it fell over the city. New Orleans went black. Throughout the country, people watched in horror, waiting for glimpses of light. The next day's news broadcasts showed water still rising, boats in the streets, and panicked residents stranded on rooftops, waiting for help. Desperation rose, and the sound of smashing windows was added to the score as stores were looted.

Paralyzed, I watched the horror unfold, tears gliding down my cheeks. The images were both familiar and strange as the stores I'd walked by on Canal Street took on new faces. Dark and damaged, the windows I'd peered into were now broken and jagged, and the shelves inside empty. Chaos engulfed the city. I tried to imagine what it must be like to live there—my eyes jolted open by fear. New Orleans—this city that welcomed me like a lover—was in terrible trouble.

As the clouds parted and the water receded, the quilt that was thrown over the city, now a ragged, soaked blanket, was slowly pulled back, revealing what remained—homes destroyed or completely washed away; streets, trees, neighborhoods, and lives uprooted. There was so much work to be done.

My heart's voice whispered, *What can I do?*

Fearless in her creativity and in her Baha'i faith, Marj Paik has been one of my greatest teachers.

# Chapter 5

The rented van bumped and jostled beneath and around us in constant vibration as we drove south. My daughter, Maddie, navigated as she and I threaded our way to New Orleans carrying fifty sewing machines. It was March 2006.

In the days after Hurricane Katrina swept the Gulf, I watched the news as dysfunction unfolded—streets in disarray, homes, neighborhoods, and whole communities destroyed. Recovery moved at a glacial pace. *Take the machines to New Orleans*, said the voice I had grown to trust. With no idea whether or when sewing machines would be needed, or by whom, I spun a plan to deliver our remaining machines to New Orleans.

I did not doubt rerouting the machines as I redirected the compass, but I felt I needed to contact the donors who had entrusted me with their funds. I called the school district, the Girl Scout leader, and the club presidents, explaining my decision. "I need to shift this effort to New Orleans. Is that okay with you and your group?" No one questioned the change in direction as I refocused on a disaster within our own borders.

Bahee was disappointed but understanding. Grateful for the twenty-five machines we had sent to Sri Lanka and India, he understood my need to change direction.

Our donors agreed that I could use their gifts to rent a cargo van and pay for gas for the trip. I called the Astor Crowne Plaza on the corner of Canal and Bourbon Streets in New Orleans and explained my plan to drive down, bringing "relief" sewing machines. I asked whether they might give me a complimentary room for a few nights. The Astor was a busy place, with displaced New Orleanians living within its walls while they tried to navigate their devastated homes and lives. Despite the Astor's burgeoning guest list, the manager agreed to gift me a room.

Squinting in the bright sunlight, I glanced at fourteen-year-old Maddie, a map draped across her knees. We'd had a rough go of it lately due to issues at school and in her private life, so our recent interactions had ranged from silent to shouting and everything in between. I'd been surprised when she accepted my invitation to ride along—fifteen hours together in the car each way. I wanted to be near her to listen to her rhythms and try to understand our impasses.

My interactions within our family had been tense in recent weeks and months. I often felt unmoored with both children testing the boundaries as they lived their teenage years and a husband building a new career path. Tears sprang forth when I least expected them, and I struggled to discern their source. My life was good by all accounts. I loved my children fiercely and was grateful for the ability to carve my life around them. But I was restless and didn't know why. I found solace in the push within me to create something of my own and lived in that solace as much as I could.

Our destination on the first night was Violet Hill, Arkansas, in the Ozark foothills, to pay a visit my sixth-grade teacher, Mrs. Paik. Our wheels crunched on the gravel as we drove the long road to the house she shared with her husband, Joe. We passed organic gardens and hand-hewn wooden fences. Marj and Joe Paik had built the house themselves, a simple concrete block structure with small windows like kind eyes looking out over the hills and gardens, offering a cozy welcome. The van crunched to a halt as Marj walked out of the house, arms open, a huge smile spread across her face.

Marj Paik was my teacher when my parents chose to take me out of public school to attend Pinewood for my sixth-grade year. This independent school was Mrs. Paik's dream: twenty-five kids from first through sixth grade working and learning together in a tiny, two-room school in Wales, Wisconsin, with Mrs. Paik at the helm. Our daily walks in the woods and frequent field trips to farms, mills, and gardens were part of the curriculum. Big kids were expected to help the "littles," and arguments were settled with thought and care. Parents stepped in to teach math and reading and music. The deepest lessons, however, didn't align with any ordinary curriculum. One lesson, in particular, stayed with me throughout my life. I could feel Mrs. Paik's hand on my shoulder as she intently looked at my sixth-grade self. "When you grow up, wait a while to get married and have kids. See the world, learn a lot. You'll have many years of standing at the kitchen sink doing dishes and looking out the window. You'll need something to think about."

I couldn't wait to see Mrs. Paik.

As we stepped out of the van, Marj pulled Maddie into her arms. "I've waited so long to know you!" she whispered. The last time Marj had "seen" Maddie, fourteen years before, my daughter had been just a bump in my belly.

Then she took me in her arms. "How are you, my dear?" Unexpected tears filled my eyes as I nestled into her generous hug. I needed to be there.

Marj ushered us inside. Her artwork dotted the walls of their simple, earth-friendly home. We ended up in Marj's studio, broad and well-lit, her jewelry and batik supplies spread over the workbenches.

"Maddie, would you like to try batik?" she asked. She cupped Maddie's hand, showing her how to hold the delicate pen, a gentle guide for stroking the wax. Gradually removing her hand, Maddie's hand continued the path on its own, her shoulders relaxed, her breathing slow and steady.

"Let the artist inside you do the work," Marj said, then nudged me, suggesting we give Maddie time alone.

The two of us walked out into the sunlight. "Would you like to see our gardens?" Marj offered. With the warmth of the sun on our skin, we walked together, two old friends. "We live off of these gardens," Marj said. An extraordinary teacher, Marj never stopped sharing her world with others, allowing those who listened to paint their own picture of what they were feeling. When she asked about my life, I shared more than expected. "I don't know where this idea came from, but I had to listen," I told her, knowing she would understand. And she did.

"Honey, you are doing just what you are supposed to be doing." Once again, tears filled my eyes as she pulled me into a hug. "You've always had courage and light inside of you, although I don't think you always see it," she whispered. "Keep on going."

When we returned to the studio, we paused outside the window to watch Maddie at work. She dipped her pen into the wax slowly and carefully, drawing on the handmade paper. Her body and breathing moved rhythmically with the design.

"We've been having some troubles lately, Maddie and I," I confided.

"Ah, my girl, it'll smooth out," Marj said quietly. "Sometimes the best thing is to say nothing. Just be there for her and love her up."

The next morning, we said our goodbyes to Marj and Joe.

"I'm so happy to see you again," I whispered as Marj held me close.

"You're still my favorite flavor," she said. I felt her smiling against my wet cheek. Marj and Joe stood with arms around each other and waved as we climbed into the van and pulled away from the house, prepared for the final leg of our journey.

We settled into day two of the drive, winding through Arkansas' soft mountain passes, a corner of Tennessee, Memphis, and the big river, and then down through Mississippi with its lush green—a welcome sight after our Wisconsin winter. Louisiana's swamps and bogs, Spanish moss, and mysterious inlets greeted us. A question dotted my inner landscape: *Would anyone want our cargo?*

Rainer Maria Rilke famously wrote about working with the unknown:

"Be patient toward all that is unsolved in your heart and try to love the questions themselves, like locked rooms and like books that are now written in a very foreign tongue. Do not now seek the answers, which cannot be given you because you would not be able to live them. And the point is, to live everything. Live the questions now. Perhaps you will then gradually, without noticing it, live along some distant day into the answer."

When I had needed a connection in Sri Lanka, I held the question, and my answer arrived in a phone call from a friend. Pam introduced me to Bahee. Similarly, I wondered who I would connect with in New Orleans. Once again, I held the question. And once again, a friend reached out with an answer. When Deb called and asked whether I needed a contact person in New Orleans, I smiled and wrote down the information she shared. Her brother-in-law, Walter, was the rector at Grace Episcopal Church on Canal Street. He had agreed to announce our upcoming visit during the service on the Sunday before we arrived. Though the church had seen four feet of water, the church community was still meeting in a building down the street. I only hoped that someone had heard his message.

We arrived in New Orleans late in the day, checking into our hotel and placing the van in the hands of the valet. Though tired, we changed our clothes and headed out into the springtime air and the French Quarter.

Walking down Bourbon Street, we spied two palm readers on either side of a large iron gate. "Do you want your palm read?" I asked Maddie. She sat down across from a weathered, wise woman who gently turned over Maddie's hand. "Oh, honey," the palm reader said, shaking her head, "you've really gotten into it lately." Maddie was quiet. "Looks like you've been in some trouble. You'll be needing to take the back seat for a while." Maddie looked over her shoulder at me, the uncomfortable truth hovering. "Maybe I'll go and have my palm read, too," I said, stepping away so she could hear the rest privately.

I walked over to the other palm reader and sat down. She held my hands gently in both of hers. "Well, honey," she said, "looks like you're in the middle of something." Her eyes met mine. "It's big, bigger than you know. I don't think you can see how big it is yet." My heart buzzed. "You have people watching over you," she said. "You have everything you need."

The next morning, I eased the van alongside Grace Episcopal Church, where Reverend Walter awaited us. He gave us a brief tour of the gutted church, describing its pre-storm look and their plans

36

for reconstruction. Tired and cavernous, with a visible four-foot waterline across the front, the church had clearly seen a struggle. We set up folding tables to hold the fifty machines, creating a makeshift vintage sewing machine display in the gutted sanctuary.

Then we waited.

People filtered in, parishioners and neighbors, one by one, and wandered among the machines. Talk focused on what they wished to sew, and I guided each person to a machine appropriate to their needs. Everyone carried stories about the storm and unfathomable loss. Tales of lives uprooted—some literally washed away—and the feeling that the country had moved on, leaving New Orleans behind. I listened as each story painted a picture of yet another situation where hope was hard to find. But it was there. A woman wearing a Kelly green vest and Mardi Gras beads said, "Just when we think hope is lost, someone like you comes along and brings hope back."

Among the visitors and the curious was a woman named Becky. Well dressed and confident, Becky stood out. She looked at the lineup of machines. When I asked her what she might need, she said, "I'm looking for machines for the Mardi Gras Indians," and explained a bit about this culture, unique to New Orleans. The Indians create suits each year for their traditional celebrations and ceremonies. While the suits they create are largely handmade with elaborate bead and feather designs, they need machines to sew sections together. Those few machines that were shared throughout the community had mostly been lost in the storm.

"Would you consider giving me more than one?" Becky asked. She walked away with three. I suggested she return at the end of the day in case there were any more remaining.

Slowly and consistently, people arrived, taking time to share their stories and select a sewing machine. Many asked, "Why are you doing this?" or "Are these really free?"

"I just thought you might need a sewing machine," I said, and "Yes, they are free—please take one."

The notion that sewing machines hold keys to healing is firmly rooted within me. A sewer for most of my life, I know the joy of creating and the freedom of thought that comes when my hands are busy. I believed with every fiber that these machines could help.

I had not considered making more than one visit to New Orleans. I thought we would share the machines we had collected and then return home, wrapping up what I thought was a chapter in my life. Little by little, during our day at Grace Church, I realized, through a story, a look, or a hug, that I was not wrapping something up but rather just beginning. The palm reader's words came back to me. "It's big, bigger than you know. I don't think you can see how big it is yet." I had no idea what would come next, but I knew this wasn't over. I knew I needed to get back home and find more machines.

At the end of the day, seven machines were left, and Becky arrived, ready to take them.

"I'm going to be delivering these to some really great women tomorrow," Becky said. "Would you like to come along?" Maddie looked skeptical, and I heartily agreed. "Great," said Becky. "I'll pick you both up at your hotel at ten."

She said, "Just when I think there's no hope left, someone like you comes along and brings hope back."

# Chapter 6

The bar's loud exterior caught me by surprise. Images of Ernie K-Doe and his wife, Antoinette, greeted us before Antoinette even opened the door. It was Sunday morning, and we arrived with Becky for the first of our deliveries.

The Mother-in-Law Lounge on North Claiborne Avenue in New Orleans is a community landmark. Opened in 1994 as a bar and showcase for the legendary Ernie K-Doe, Miss Antoinette kept it open after Ernie died in 2001. The Mother-in-Law was not just a bar but a community hub that offered a place for a wide variety of groups. Krewes, bands, and organizers of all stripes relied on Miss Antoinette for space and support—and often a delicious meal of rice and beans. A mannequin of Ernie sat perched on a shelf in his royal "King of the World" attire, presiding over all.

Katrina brought five and a half feet of water into the aging structure. Antoinette had taken the mannequin of Ernie, thrown it into the back of the hearse she drove, and left town. Returning as soon as it was safe, Antoinette vowed to reopen the bar. She shared this story with us as we stood in the shadows of the gutted interior.

"I knew I wanted to reopen, but I wasn't sure how that would work," Antoinette told us. When the Hands-on Network offered to help, Antoinette gratefully accepted. Looking around the place, I could see it was already on its way to recovery. Miss Antoinette was optimistic. "I've got help," she said as she described the efforts of every group and individual who had shown up to share her burden.

Miss Antoinette told us about the Baby Dolls, social clubs with deep roots, to which she'd belonged for years. Miss Antoinette sewed her own costumes and helped many of her neighbors finish theirs. She sewed souvenirs—pillows bearing Ernie's likeness—that she sold in the bar to raise funds. She was thrilled when we offered her the powerful, second-hand Pfaff sewing machine to continue her work. "Could I have a couple more?" she asked. She knew of others in the neighborhood who could use machines.

"Of course!" I replied.

"I love to sew!" she said. "I can set this up upstairs, and it'll take my mind off the mess down here!" Though packed with rescued items from the club downstairs, her upstairs apartment was homey. I could easily imagine her finding peace as her hands were busy sewing.

Our next stop was Joyce Montana's home, a blue and white double shotgun. Joyce, like Miss Antoinette, is New Orleans royalty. The widow of Big Chief Tootie Montana, Joyce was his muse and "right hand." She welcomed us in and asked if we'd like to see some of Tootie's suits. Rescued from the rising waters of Katrina's flood, the suits were beyond remarkable—our first brush with the actual costumes of the Mardi Gras Indians—brilliant colors, taller than tall, with headdresses of feathers and beads. Joyce walked along with us, describing the process of creating the suits. She told us there were many lean years when the cost of building a new suit was unaffordable; often, one year's suit was dismantled right after Mardi Gras to use the beads and feathers for a new suit in another year. Joyce described the hours, weeks, and months of beading that went into each suit. Her head nodded as if bearing a great weight as she shared how heavy the headdresses were and the challenge of wearing them for several hours. Tootie had died just a year before while addressing the City Council about the treatment of Mardi Gras Indians. Joyce's pride radiated. We thanked her, leaving four machines for her to share with her community.

Saying goodbye to Joyce, we climbed back into the car with Becky, who took us on a long tour of the different wards, showing us the area affected most by the flood. FEMA markings dotted the houses. Forming an X shape, the top block of the mark showed the date the house was checked, and the left block was signed by the task force that inspected the house. The right quadrant included special instructions, and the bottom block recorded how many people were found in the house. Vines snaked up the sides of buildings, and mold cast a speckled veil over all. We spanned the bridge into the Lower Ninth Ward. Slowly making our way through the rugged roads, we skirted around potholes so deep they could swallow a car. The Lower Ninth was a monument to death and destruction. The force of the wind and water had overturned trucks and tossed boats onto rooftops, crushing some houses. Many homes were simply washed away, leaving driveways leading nowhere, ghostly reminders of what had been. I was at once torn between wanting to look and feeling as if I was intruding on something sacred. One pile of debris had a teddy bear sitting atop, eyes hanging on threads—a sad sentry guarding the area.

I was glad Becky was driving; I was distracted by the view in every direction. The storm washed away most street signs and many landmarks, so navigation by the uninitiated was nearly impossible. I drank it all in, one street after another—house, vacant lot, mold, FEMA marks, silently witnessing. Driving down one street with cars parked every which way, Becky looked in the rearview mirror and muttered, "Oh shit." A police car was following us, and Becky pulled over. "Don't say anything," Becky warned. "The cops are scarier than anyone around here right now."

The policeman stuck his head in the window. "Is there a problem, officer?" Becky asked. "You're going the wrong way," he said.

"I didn't see a one-way sign," Becky replied, shrugging her shoulders.

"Well, it *is* one way," he said, his face a warning.

In a place that felt like the Wild West, with cars pointed in every direction, there was no way to know. Lawlessness and destruction were the norm. I turned to Maddie in the back seat, "You okay, honey?" Maddie silently nodded.

When Becky dropped us off later that day, we had few words left. The city had taken them and, at the same time, busted my mind wide open. Color and mud, beads and moss, the city was a spectrum, at once overwhelming and intoxicating.

That evening, Maddie and I walked again through the French Quarter, the same but different after our day. The rules were new, and we both were jangly. To calm Maddie (and myself), I recited my most basic rules for traveling in a new place, as much a reminder to myself as to her. Stay where it's lit, stay with groups, and don't wander off on dark streets alone. When in doubt, stay with what you know.

But the world of what I knew was shifting under my feet, becoming broader and much more colorful. Intending to make this trip, deliver machines, come back home, and resume life as I'd known it was no longer possible. Life was no longer the way I'd known it. I felt that to my core. And while I knew this was true, I did not know what it meant. I didn't know what would come next. I only knew that I needed more sewing machines.

We lined up machines for each distribution and more often than not, folks would say, "This is just like the one I lost!"

# Chapter 7

The darkness of the television studio at once held and frightened me. I shifted my weight, my feet searching for stability on the high stool where I was perched.

"We'll start in just a minute," the news anchor said. "Are you ready?" I searched my face on the monitor behind him, seeing my jitters revealed. Could anyone else feel how nervous I was?

It was September 2006. Martha, the church secretary at Grace Church, had sent out a press release announcing my arrival. My second trip to New Orleans, this time accompanied by my husband, Walt, driving the familiar rented cargo van. We carried eighty-five machines.

In response to Martha's press release, I received a call from WGNO, one of the local television stations. They had invited me for an interview on the morning news once we arrived in New Orleans.

It had been six months since my March trip with Maddie. Sewing machines continued to arrive at Hans', and my little team prepared them for their next chapter. We planned another sewing machine distribution at Grace Episcopal Church.

With microphones on and cameras focused, the interview began. Speaking to the reporter, eyes fixed on the monitor, I described the idea, the path so far, and the distribution I'd planned for that day. I watched my face and saw confidence. As far as I could tell, there was no outward sign of the knot that twisted in my stomach. A line of text scrolled the bottom of the screen, "Free sewing machines. Saturday. Grace Episcopal Church. Sunday, Mother-in-Law Lounge." My breath caught with a twinge of anxiety.

I had talked with Miss Antoinette before leaving Wisconsin.

"Miss Antoinette, I'd like to bring some machines over to your bar on Sunday. I'm concerned that some of the people in your neighborhood may not be able to get to the big distribution on Saturday. Would that be okay?"

"Of course, honey," she purred in her silky southern voice.

I planned to take whatever we didn't give away on Saturday to the bar on Sunday. Hopefully, between the two venues, we would distribute all eighty-five machines.

Walt and I wove through the French Quarter and Canal Street from the television studio to the church. We passed piles of insulation, trash, and rusting appliances still stacked on the curb—remnants of the storm from over a year before. Approaching Grace Church, I did a double take. People were gathered on the lawn and lined up along the street, talking with each other as they stood beneath the canopy of Canal Street's ancient trees.

We pulled up at the side of the church and were met by Martha.

"Oh my," she said. "There are already hundreds of people here!"

And there were.

With an hour remaining before the distribution, Walt and I began unloading the machines. Men waiting in line stepped up to help. We set up our sewing machine giveaway in a little chapel on the river side of the church.

Clearly, there were more people than machines. I recalled my conversation with Miss Antoinette and my promise to her.

"Let's save fifteen machines in the van for tomorrow," I said, leaving us with seventy.

Turning to walk into the chapel, I was met by a red-haired woman intent on talking with me.

"My name is Sheila Stroup, and I write for the *Times-Picayune.* I'd love to do a story about you and your sewing machines."

We opened the doors at nine, and the distribution began. I walked to the head of the line and waved my arms to get everyone's attention.

"Hi, and welcome," I said. "I'm glad to see you all. I'm not sure we will have enough machines, but we'll do the best we can."

The line began to move. One by one, eager sewers and I greeted one another as they stepped inside the chapel. Martha took their names. Sheila grabbed moments with people here and there to hear their stories.

"What kind of sewing do you like to do?" I would ask as we walked together toward the machines. The language of sewing traverses all.

"Oh Lord, this is just like the one I lost!" a woman exclaimed as we approached the table. She placed her hands on a heavy-duty Kenmore. Like a reincarnation of a long-lost friend, the machine was clearly the one for her. Walt helped her get it to her car. One by one, machines were scooped up and taken to their new homes. Martha and I looked out over the remaining crowd as the last few machines disappeared. Hundreds of people still stood outside of the church.

"I'll get some index cards!" Martha said and headed off to the church office.

"Okay, everyone," I shouted from the church steps, "we've run out of machines, but I'll be getting more. I'm not sure when I'll be back, but I will keep bringing machines until everyone has one. Martha has index cards. I need each of you to fill out your contact information on a card so I can find you when I have a machine ready. I promise I'll be back."

Martha moved through the crowd, handing out index cards and pens. Over five hundred completed cards were collected.
"We'll wait," people said. "Thank you for remembering us."

With cards collected and the crowd leaving, Martha, Walter, Walt, Sheila, and I collapsed on the church steps in the September sun. I had gone from worrying about whether we would find homes for the machines in the van to realizing we didn't have enough. I worried that people would be angry when they left empty-handed, but found that they were patient and grateful—over five hundred people. I was already beginning to imagine my next visit.

We arrived at the Mother-in-Law Lounge at noon on Sunday, an hour before our one o'clock distribution. Approaching the bar on Claiborne Street, I did another double take as I spied a line of people waiting outside the bar and trailing down the block. We parked the van alongside the bar and got out.

"Hi, everyone. Are you here for machines?" People nodded, some leaning against the walls, others sitting on the sidewalk. Miss Antoinette kept the door to her bar locked, and I rang the doorbell. After a few moments, the door opened slightly. Miss Antoinette's arm reached out, grabbing mine.

"Get in here!" Miss Antoinette said as she pulled me inside. Walt squeezed in after me.

Antoinette blurted out, "I was watching the news yesterday morning and saw 'Free sewing machines at the Mother-in-Law Lounge on Sunday!' I almost fainted!"

She had forgotten our conversation.

"Miss Antoinette, I'm sorry this surprised you! Remember, I called you to ask if this was okay!"

She shook her head and smiled. "Well, I don't remember, honey, but it's fine. These ladies have been out there all night! They've been yelling in my mail slot, 'We know you're in there!'"

"Looks like about twenty-five people out there," I whispered, peeking out the door.

"We can do it like a lottery. I'll hand out numbers," Walt announced. Always the fair-minded meeting planner, Walt had a strategy for everything. He headed for the door.

Antoinette grabbed his arm.

"Honey, those ladies know who got here first. They're not going to like that idea."

Walt pulled ahead. "Oh, don't worry. I'll explain it to them." He reached for the door.

"Honey, no. They know who was here first. I'm going with you. I'm going to save your little white butt." And with that, Antoinette and Walt stepped into the sunlight to greet the crowd.

I organized the remaining fifteen machines in the shadows of the bar while Ernie K-Doe's mannequin peered down at me curiously from his shelf. Rumor had it that Antoinette dressed him every day.

A popular guy, groups regularly picked up Ernie's mannequin to ride along on Mardi Gras floats and to attend Saints games.

One by one, the women stepped into the bar, squinting in the darkness as they eyed the machines. The machines, perched on the bar, tables, and barstools, had transformed the room into a shadowy shop.

A woman burst in, her hair under a dye cap, a salon cape around her shoulders. "I heard you have sewing machines!" she said.

Miss Antoinette grabbed her arm and turned her around. "Loreen, you go right back to the chair and finish your dye job!" she said. "These ladies have been waiting!" Loreen shuffled out.

One by one, the fifteen machines disappeared out the door. The remaining folks filled out contact information on index cards. As the last of the machines left the building, Antoinette poured beers. "Honey, those ladies were there all night! Some said they walked over from the line at the church!"

I shook my head. "I just can't believe it," I said, taking a sip of beer. "And I wondered if we would find homes for them all!"

"What can't you believe?" she replied. "These ladies lost everything. What you are doing with these sewing machines; this is such a big gift. Of course, people will wait."

The following day, Walt and I drove back to Wisconsin, opting to devour the entire 1,500 miles in one day. Walt took the wheel for the bulk of the trip while I leaned my forehead against the cool glass of the passenger window, letting the miles slide by. Although the visit had been something we experienced together, I somehow held it alone. I couldn't find words to talk about the immensity of this idea growing throughout me. Not for lack of trying, but the words were fumbled and inadequate as if they weren't ready to tumble from my mouth. And when I would try, Walt would nod and smile, doing his best to understand. His response, like my words, felt inadequate. So I let the words and feelings live within me, not even trying to make this experience a shared one. I thought about the promises I'd made. I had told a crowd of over five hundred people that I would return and deliver sewing machines. I had promised to seek them out. And though these promises were grand against the backdrop of my daily life, they were somehow not overwhelming. I knew this was not a "we" thing. This was a "me" thing.

I smiled at Walt and found a way to limit the conversation's scope to the experiences of this trip. We laughed with amazement as we talked about the long line of people, about Miss Antoinette's arm reaching to pull me inside and me grabbing Walt's arm to pull him along. We moved into talking about what lay ahead for us, together and independently.

The path was opening for me. Though I couldn't see much beyond my next few steps, I was filled with a surprising certainty and a knowing that the path was mine to walk.

Folks arrived at distributions excited to choose a sewing machine.

# Chapter 8

Through the fall and winter of 2006, my day-to-day continued, with duties as a mother, a worker, and a friend. Through these familiar patterns, sewing machines arrived. Friends and coworkers stepped up, smiling, to help me clean machines and sort the endless supply of fabric and notions, the whir of machines like a musical accompaniment. Shelves in the back of the store held a lineup of candidates waiting to travel to their new homes.

Martha called from Grace Church in New Orleans.

"Margaret, I keep on hearing from people wondering if they could get on the list for a machine."

I continued to say yes.

We had our script down. Martha reminded people there was no timetable as she jotted each name and contact information. I watched the stack of index cards on my desk grow, each card representing a prayer for a sewing machine. I handled them gently. My son, Alec, far better with technology than I am, helped me create a spreadsheet, and

I dropped each name and accompanying contact information into the stark grid.

The details for a January 2007 trip to New Orleans fell into place, including another complimentary hotel room, this time at the Sheraton Hotel on Canal Street. With 125 machines ready, I chose a fourteen-foot truck to transport our cargo. There was no need to wonder whether we would find a home for the machines this time—we had a list over six hundred people long. In December, I began calling the names on the list, one at a time, each conversation challenging my memory to match the voice with one of the hundreds of people I'd met on that September day only months before.

"Hi, this is Margaret. Remember that day back in September when you stood in line for a sewing machine? I'm coming down in January. Do you still need one? You do? Okay. We'll be at Grace Episcopal on Saturday, January 27, at 9 a.m. No, you don't need to bring anything. Just come. We'll see you there." As the snow swirled outside of my window in Wisconsin, I heard the siren song and warmth of New Orleans.

My coworker Julie was excited to ride along this time. A great resource, Julie knew sewing and sewing machines. On the Wednesday before our scheduled distribution date, with our coworkers' help, we loaded the truck in Madison and prepared for the drive to New Orleans.

At five that afternoon, after a long workday, we tossed our suitcases into what little space was left in the back of the truck and got on the road. We drove to St. Louis that first evening in driving snow, arriving around eleven. We would finish the trip the next day.

"You'll need to park across the street in that vacant lot," the desk clerk told us, eyeing our truck through the window of the St. Louis Sheraton. "That truck is too high for our ramp."

Julie waited in the lobby while I jockeyed the truck across the street and into the snowy parking lot. I struggled to make out the lines separating the parking spaces and pulled up as neatly as possible alongside another car. Breathing a sigh of relief and exhaustion, I dropped the keys into my jacket pocket, imagining the cozy bed awaiting me in our hotel room. The snow didn't let up.

At six the next morning, our room phone rang. My hand slapped the nightstand, searching for the receiver.

"Good morning, Ma'am. We are wondering if you have a truck parked across the street?" The words were fuzzy as I struggled to open my heavy eyes.

"What? Yes."

"Well, Ma'am, we need you to go to the truck right now and talk to the police."

"What?" I mumbled. "POLICE?"

"Yes, Ma'am. Right. Now." I brushed my teeth, threw on my jacket over my pajamas, and pulled on my boots. Separating the blinds with my fingers, I peeked into the darkness outside. It had been snowing all night.

I rode the elevator with the professionally dressed morning business crowd, my hair in a tangle, pajama bottoms peeking out between the hem of my jacket and the tops of my boots. I kept my eyes low. Cold air pierced the thin fabric around my legs as I spun through the hotel's revolving door and crossed the street. Our truck was alone in the lot, surrounded by police cars and officers, talking and watching my approach.

"Is this your truck?"

"Yes."

"Can you open the back, please?"

"Okay. Sure. Why?"

"Ma'am, we have no record of this vehicle having permission to park here."

*Huh? But the guy at the desk last night . . . so late.* My brain hurt.

"Ma'am, please open the back of the truck." I began connecting the dots—*a fourteen-foot Budget rental truck with Oklahoma plates I'd not even noticed, no record of its arrival, parked solo in a vacant lot in the middle of a big city. Timothy McVeigh. Oklahoma. 2005. Wow, me? Really?*

I fumbled with my keys and opened the padlock, shivering as the wind whipped and nipped my legs. I leaned on the clip releasing the lock, and the door rumbled up, opening the back for viewing.

"It's sewing machines," I said. "I'm taking them to New Orleans." The officers shone their flashlights into the cavernous truck with its layers of machines.

"Well, okay, Ma'am. Thank you."

"I'll be leaving in an hour or so," I said.

The officers seemed relieved to know that this pajama-clad terrorist would soon vacate the city.

I closed the truck and walked back to the hotel. Julie was waiting for the story. Now thoroughly wide awake, we got on the road earlier than expected and headed for New Orleans. We drove all day, the town markers whipping by as we traversed the states, and arrived in New Orleans around five that afternoon.

"You'll need to park the truck across the street. It won't fit in our ramp," the valet informed us as we pulled up to the front of the New Orleans Sheraton.

His statement was all too familiar. We climbed back into the truck and followed the directions to a public lot a block down busy Canal Street. Pulling into the driveway, I paused. Here? There didn't appear to be an inch of space available—and a fourteen-foot truck? I had my doubts.

"Yep, I have a spot for you," the attendant said, pointing to the postage-stamp-sized slot near the back of the lot.

"No way. I can't fit in there," I replied skeptically.

He eyed up the truck. "Sure, you'll fit just fine. It's best if you back in. I'll help you."

He guided me expertly through the cars toward my spot while I muttered under my breath, "No way, no way."

"Come on, come on," my guide shouted, wagging his fingers.

I laughed with delight as I moved the final few feet, wedging into the parking spot—in reverse! With a proud little laugh, I switched off the ignition and dropped the keys into my bag.

We were given a sweet room with two cozy beds and a view of the river. We dropped our bags, washed our faces, and headed out into the New Orleans evening. Redfish, oysters, stale beer, and the river met our noses. Music poured out of the clubs, and beads dripped from the balconies. Snugging up to the bar at the Acme Oyster House, we ordered a beer and toasted our arrival. We watched as the nimble oyster shuckers worked their magic behind the bar. The Acme is known for its oysters, the ever-present crowd, and the line out the door.

This visit carried a broad agenda and a short timeframe. The next morning we got organized. Our first stop was visiting a little girl named Keisha, a first grader with dreams of "masking" as a Mardi Gras Indian. "Masking" designates those within the Mardi Gras

Indian culture who put the time, creativity, and work into creating a suit for the Mardi Gras season. A very special machine awaited Keisha in the truck—a little green Janome with a Hello Kitty insignia. The little machine was strong and capable, despite its small size. We headed to Keisha's elementary school and knocked at her classroom door. Keisha's teacher called her over to meet us, and we knew at once it was a match. The surprise and glee in her bright eyes left no doubt. Months before, a woman had stopped into Hans' and eyed up the little Hello Kitty sewing machines. She made a donation to purchase three machines, asking that they go to children in New Orleans.

"Hi, Keisha," I said, crouching to meet her eyes. "I hear you would like to sew suits and mask with the Indians."

She nodded shyly.

The little green machine brought a heart-melting smile, and I knew I was exactly where I was supposed to be, kneeling in front of a little girl, offering a sewing machine.

"Thank you," Keisha said as her teacher helped her tuck the machine into the back of the classroom. I took her tiny hand and looked her right in the eyes. "I know you'll be a good sewer," I said. "I hope I can see one of your suits someday." Keisha nodded.

We arrived at the church at seven thirty the following morning to set up for distribution day. This time, I knew who was coming, thanks to my spreadsheet. I parked the big truck alongside the church, leaned on the hitch, and pushed open the back door. Julie and I unloaded 125 sewing machines and lined them up on tables in the little chapel. Boxes of fabric, zippers, buttons, thread, rulers, and all kinds of trim were arranged, rummage sale style, on side tables.

As I stepped outside, I noticed Sheila Stroup heading toward the chapel.

"Margaret!" she waved as she approached. "We had such a good response to that first story I wanted to do a follow-up!" After hugging Sheila, I continued on with my clipboard to address the crowd out front. The line of people filled the walkway to the church and extended down Canal Street.

"Hi, everyone. I'm Margaret. Please get with me and give me your name so I can check you off the list. When it's your turn, we'll start by finding the right sewing machine for you. You'll also notice fabric and sewing supplies along the side. You're welcome to take what you can use but look around at how many people there are here. Please leave enough for everyone."

A heavy-set woman bustled out of line and up next to me. "Did y'all hear that?" she shouted at twice my volume. "It's like the Lord says, 'Take just what you need and leave something for everyone else.'" Uh-huh, the crowd nodded. She's right. There will be enough for everyone.

All morning, people arrived, carrying birth certificates, passports, and driver's licenses, offering any means of identification they could find.

"Don't worry about it," I would say. "If I gave you a call, you're good. Let's talk about what kind of sewing you want to do." And we did. The line moved orderly and calmly. Machines for mending, machines for tailors, machines for costuming, machines for making a FEMA trailer feel more like a home. There were as many stories as people who walked through the door, and we listened to every one, for sewing is filled with our stories and memories. People would spot a machine that was just like the one they lost. Midway through the morning, a woman rode in on a motorized scooter.

"I live a mile away!" she said. "I drove this thing all the way. I can't wait to start sewing. We lost everything in the storm."

People gathered their machines and offered thank yous, asking how they could repay us for the gift of a sewing machine, and I was at a loss for words. Being able to do this work is such a gift; there is nothing I need. I searched my heart for an answer, finding it waiting.

"You can pay it forward," I said. "Pay it forward in a sewing-related way."

"I'll teach my neighbor to sew!"

"I'll share my machine!"

"I'll make blankets for the babies at the local hospital!"

"I'll mend for my neighbors."

I'll pay it forward.

That evening, in happy exhaustion, Julie and I talked over the day. The machines were gone, and the truck was exchanged for a much more manageable compact car. The pay-it-forward idea, a spur-of-the-moment suggestion, felt right, and I quietly delighted at how readily this answer appeared. Not only would this give people a way of showing gratitude, but it would also give our work a ripple effect. Paying it forward is empowering, as it promotes the idea that everyone, no matter their circumstances, has a responsibility and power to help mend their community.

At the lobby bar later that evening, I struck up a conversation with the guy next to me. With a shock of red hair and an easy smile, he asked what brought me to New Orleans, and I told him about the previous day and the distribution. My enthusiasm bubbled over.

"Wow, that's so cool! I'd love to help you," he said. "Maybe I could send you a machine. My daughter is looking at a new one. Maybe I could send you the one she has. What is your web address?"

"We don't have a website," I replied, thinking about the lined pads of paper and the box of index cards that held every bit of information about the organization, a system that had served me well so far. It had never dawned on me that we would need a website.

"No website?" he replied, eyebrows raised. "You need one! That's how I will help you. I'll put you in touch with my web guy and pay him to design a website for you."

Two days later, Julie and I boarded a plane back to Wisconsin, plans for collecting the next set of machines already spinning in my head. We had impacted 125 lives with this batch of machines, and who knows how many more as those people paid it forward. When I arrived home, I quickly began working on a logo and website plans, thanks to a connection with a red-haired guy named James. My coworker Rebecca penned a logo as I described the image in my head. A sewing machine with hands giving it one to another, a heart under the needle. Giving and receiving. A picture with a message: here is a tool that can change lives.

Cherice Harrison Nelson and her mother, Herreast Harrison, have been integral to our work in the New Orleans community.

# Chapter 9

"I will tell you my response, and this is solely what I believe. I don't speak for anyone else. I believe this tradition is an homage to the mutual struggles of First Nation, Native Americans, people of African descent, black folks, African American—whatever they may want to be called—but it's an homage to the mutual struggle for freedom and self-actualization. This tradition is a living testament that people of African descent did not forget their ancestral homeland. We remember, and these memories include the ceremonial dress, narrative beadwork, feather artistry that are part of the color and light of the culture.

Many think it is cloaked in the feathers and the finery. I think that it is not cloaked. I feel that it is really not a masquerade. It's putting forth your authentic self. That's what I feel I do. When I wear traditional Western clothes, that is the masquerade. That is what I wear to fit into this Western society. The ritual attire that I create when I come out on Mardi Gras Day is what I choose."

–CHERICE HARRISON-NELSON IN A 2013 INTERVIEW

The air hung thick with chicory and milk foam as my eyes searched the room for a table. I'd never met Cherice. Scanning the shadowy corners of CC's Coffee House on Magazine Street in New Orleans' Garden District, I spotted a table and prepared to meet her.

"You need to get with Cherice Harrison-Nelson," Becky had said. "Cherice is a Mardi Gras Indian and an important voice in the community. There is a lot of need there. Cherice can connect you with the people who need sewing machines."

We'd met, Becky and I, each time I visited New Orleans, ever since that first encounter at the church in March 2006. Becky was a light of welcome, a familiar face in a city that still felt unfamiliar. She educated me. Not a native New Orleanian but living part of each year in the city, she was involved enough to have a sense of the city's pulse and who I should meet.

A tall, regal woman stood in the doorway, her head wrapped in a bright African print gele. Our eyes met, and she made her way through the maze of tables, carefully setting down her bag and seating herself comfortably. The strength of her presence made me want to put my absolute best foot forward.

We introduced ourselves, and I described The Sewing Machine Project—the machines, the trips, and the call to continue. Cherice raised her eyes to mine, her gaze intent.

"The Indians could use machines," she said, taking a sip of her coffee, steam rising like a plume between her eyebrows.

"I don't know much about the culture," I offered, feeling a sudden need for transparency. "Becky has told me a little."

Cherice began. Accounts of the origins of the Mardi Gras Indians are as varied as the many groups that exist. Their suits tell personal stories of history and struggle, triumph and power in their designs. New suits are created every year by masking Indians. Much of the year is filled with the planning and hand beading—so detailed and intricate.

Cherice looked at me across the table.

"We work on them all year long," she said. "Panels are beaded by hand, but there is also plenty of machine work to be done. The panels need to be connected. Ruffles are more easily made on a machine, and a soft undersuit is made to protect the skin. We need machines for all of this," she explained.

"Could we work together?" I asked. "I have lots of machines to offer."

It was the spring of 2007 as we sat at the coffeehouse, getting to know one another and working out the details of my next visit. While I still had names to check off my list, I agreed that each of my deliveries would include some machines for the Indians. Cherice collected the names of those needing them, offering machines only to Indians who were currently masking. I provided the tools.

And so it began, a relationship built on mutual trust and respect that would continue many years into the future. I delivered heavier "workhorse" machines, and Cherice and I coordinated the deliveries. On the appointed day, I hauled the machines to a distribution point—often Cherice's or her mother's home—and the intended recipients arrived one by one. Cherice introduced each person along with their role in their group. As we talked, I listened to the new ways these machines would bring meaning—creating art and celebrating rituals—and we would choose a machine together that was best suited for their purposes. We would lift each lid to reveal the tool beneath, reviewing features and capabilities. One by one, the machines disappeared as new doors opened.

In the moments in between, I learned more about Cherice and her mother, Mrs. Harrison. Beacons in the community, both are educators in every aspect of their lives. Cherice, a scholar in her own right, has taught elementary school and university courses. Mrs. Harrison, a retired educator, has created a foundation that has given thousands of books to children. Together, they have created the Guardians Institute and Donald Harrison, Sr. Cultural Museum, a community resource named after Cherice's father, furthering cultural traditions.

Cherice stepped into my path and became my teacher. We stood together at the Super Sunday parade, watching the Mardi Gras Indians display their incredible suits. A quiet voice in my ear, Cherice coached me on the proper way to address masking Indians, etiquette I wouldn't otherwise have known. She invited me to the funeral of a revered Indian chief, simply letting me know about the service and suggesting I might want to be there. And I was, stepping into the second line, waving a white handkerchief, along with hundreds of others, to the rhythm of a brass band through the streets of New Orleans.

Mrs. Harrison has been a teaching voice in each of our encounters, sharing stories of her history and that of her late husband, Big Chief Donald Harrison. She has educated me, quietly but insistently. I witnessed her love in action when I attended one of her many book distributions at a local elementary school. "Some of these children have never had a brand-new book," she told me as she explained her foundation and its mission.

Cherice and Mrs. Harrison are a powerful force in the New Orleans community, stressing literacy and education, respect for cultural tradition, and deep regard for their roots. They've had a powerful impact on me. As guides along my path, they have scooped me up and opened my eyes to experiences I would otherwise have missed.

They have moved me to see and know the people I serve, all with grace, dignity, and mutual respect.

We do not walk our path alone. My gratitude pours forth for the teachers we are given. Through listening and saying yes, we open ourselves to all they offer. I bow in the deepest respect to these impactful, wise, and resonant guides, shining a light on all we need to learn.

The day of the Kegger dawned bright and sunny, and was matched by the mood of all who attended.

# Chapter 10

"Margaret, we need to talk about a few things." Joe looked up at me as we sorted donation checks. It was the summer of 2007, and I had just returned from New Orleans and my first meeting with Cherice.

I'd met Joe when I was invited to make a presentation to a Wisconsin Kiwanis Club two years earlier. At their meeting, the president surprised everyone by suggesting they collect donations. Coins plinked against the metal edges of the bowl as it moved through the crowd, tinny music punctuating the post-meeting conversation. An older gentleman made his way over to me and touched my arm.

"My name is Joe. I'm the club treasurer," he'd said. "I'm guessing your organization is not a 501c3."

I nodded.

"If you like, your donations can be funneled through our club. That way, donors can receive a tax advantage for giving you money. I am an accountant. I will keep track of your donations, and we can meet monthly to review the record and make deposits."

The kindness of strangers had become familiar, so I gratefully agreed, and Joe and I worked this way for a year and a half. Donations sent to me were first carefully recorded and tallied by Joe. I wrote the thank you notes and made the deposits. I looked forward to our monthly meetings over coffee, always curious to see if we'd received any donations, but even more, enjoying our respectful working connection and all that Joe was teaching me about proper recordkeeping.

When Joe said we had some things to discuss, my mind went directly to worry. Had I done something wrong? I looked across the table into Joe's kind eyes.

"You're getting more and more donations, and that's good," he said, smiling. "You must be doing something right. Given what you are taking in, I think you have some decisions to make. You need to form your own nonprofit or find another umbrella group under which to operate. Your donations are becoming more than the Kiwanis Club and I can help manage."

For three years, I worked steadily to guide The Sewing Machine Project, managing volunteers, plans, and money. I was always thinking about and making arrangements for the next delivery. Next steps came naturally as doors opened and opportunities presented themselves. But this was a bigger leap. Nonetheless, my answer came easily.

"I'll create my own 501c3," I said.

"I can connect you with an attorney who can help," Joe said, smiling, "but really give this some thought. Consider it carefully. You are at a tipping point. Taking the step to become a nonprofit is a big one."

I called my friend, Bob. A source of encouragement and advice since that first TV interview, I trusted Bob's opinion. "Well, Margie," Bob said, "this is a big decision. You are considering the trajectory of an organization. This decision means you are committing to growth, to staying with this. Is this where you want to put your time and energy?" My "yes" rose immediately.

Within weeks, I sat across from Peter, a local land trust attorney who specialized in nonprofits. Peter described the process and the work involved. I would need to complete a lot of paperwork, carefully considering the organization's bylaws and rules. I would need to build a board of directors. And, of course, there was his fee. Though dramatically discounted, the price tag was still more than I could afford. The money I had already raised was off-limits, designated for getting machines where they needed to go. Money to cover legal fees would need to be raised separately. The $3,000 price tag hovered in the air like an unanswered question. We agreed to start the paperwork, a familiar assurance emanating from my depths. *I can find the money.*

Sitting on the front porch that weekend, I shared these developments with my friend Martha, spring's sharp nip still in the air. It was April 2007.

"Where will you get the money, Margie?" Martha asked.

"I don't know," I said. "I need to raise $3,000."

"Ooh, that's a lot. Maybe we should throw a kegger." Martha smiled, half joking. "It worked in college."

My laughter subsided when I looked into Martha's face. She was serious.

"I mean it, Margie," she said. "We could do it this summer. We could raise at least part of the money."

And I began to believe her.

I once again called upon Bob and shared the idea. "Bob, we thought we could throw a kegger to raise money for the legal fees. Would you be able to get some beer donated from the Great Dane?" Bob's position as a partner in our local brewpub could prove useful. "I'll check, Margie," Bob said. "I'm pretty sure I can."

I called my neighbor across the street to share the idea. Tori and her husband, Dennis, own a historic home on Lake Monona. "We were thinking we could throw a kegger. Any chance we could do it in your beautiful yard?" Without hesitation, they agreed, and we set to making arrangements.

I called Rob, a high school friend. His marketing company agreed to create and donate custom T-shirts and hats sporting our logo that we could offer for sale.

We were on our way.

I sent postcards to everyone I knew—and many people I'd yet to meet—inviting them for a Saturday in June, and then I prayed for a sunny day. That Saturday morning dawned sunny and warm. Once again, I wondered for a moment if anyone would come, a familiar refrain that accompanied each leap of faith.

And people came. Under a sweeping white tent, sides open to let the breezes in, folks laughed and talked. Potluck dishes lined the tables. The beer was ice cold. Everyone sported neon green wristbands they had purchased upon arrival from my son and his high school friends positioned at the entrance.

That evening, I stood perched on the stone steps of the patio in the glow of the evening and the warmth of so many kind souls and spoke to the group. I thanked everyone for coming, for their kindness and support, and for helping us toward our $3,000 goal. A voice rose from the back.

"How much have we raised so far?" The "we" resounded in the air. We were a collective, and it felt good. People were invested in the fundraiser's success.

"Around $1,800," I said, noting our last count.

"Pass the hat!" someone shouted. A bowl, emptied of pretzels, made its way through the crowd. Voices, laughter, and the rustling of new leaves in the summer breeze filled the air. The bowl traveled, hand to hand, with very little sound, bills and checks, rather than coins, filling its tinny interior. The bowl was finally passed to me, filled to the brim, and I passed it to Tori.

Tori and Dennis took the money inside to count. All eyes were on Tori when she returned, smiling. "We're at $2,900!" she shouted, and everyone cheered.

"We only need $100 more!" someone exclaimed.

"I've got it!" a voice rang, and a check quickly made its way to me.

I stepped down from the stone wall but didn't feel like I was on solid ground. I was floating. Moving through the crowd, I hugged everyone I could reach, wiping my happy tears. The sun was setting, casting a warm glow over the lawn, the tent, the faces before me. No one wanted to leave, so we lit a bonfire and circled our chairs around. Voices, quieter now in the dimming light, held the excitement of the day. I looked across at Peter, and he lifted his glass. I looked around the circle and into the faces of this community that had come together around an idea that had asked to be made real.

In the weeks that followed, Peter and I got busy with the details and paperwork. We used templates to write the bylaws, refining them to reflect what I wanted The Sewing Machine Project to be. Grateful for Peter's experience in structuring nonprofits, I was amazed at the tiny details we needed to address, keenly aware that I would have overlooked them on my own. Peter reminded me that I would need to assemble a board. "It won't have to be big," he said.

In the quiet of my thoughts, I pulled together the simplest of parameters for my first board of directors—people who held a genuine interest in this effort and who hadn't doubted it could be done. I called Bob, who heartily agreed to be my first board member. I talked to Katie, a retired teacher and sewer whom I'd met through my work at Hans'. I called Bob Heideman, whom I'd met at a Kiwanis club meeting and had instantly formed a connection. Bob and his wife, Caroll, had made financial donations to The Sewing Machine Project and believed in the power of small groups to change the world. They both joined the board.

And this is how we began. Our group of five met monthly for breakfast and considered all that impacted the budding organization. Wise, thoughtful, careful, and frugal, the group helped me structure my dreamlike approach into tangible steps. As new opportunities and possibilities arrived, they helped me to make them real.

When I asked if I could take a picture of the Quilters, they each chose one of their creations to wrap themselves.

# Chapter 11

The sign read, "Work for God, please." Perched in a tree, about six feet off the ground, the small sign was barely visible through the ivy that wound and curled around the branches. I slowed the rental car to a stop, the gravel crunching on the narrow shoulder as I shifted into reverse and backed up. The road, a twisted thread through a hardwood forest, pushed my eyes to stay alert, its curves requiring attention. The sign called me. I slowed the car and backed up to take a picture. I was on my way to Gee's Bend, Alabama.

Months before, my brother and his wife shared details of a recent road trip they had taken from the East Coast to New Orleans. They had stopped in Gee's Bend, a destination one must seek with intention since its location in the crook of the Alabama River is rarely stumbled upon. They had gone to find the quilters.

The idea struck a chord. It hummed. I had visited the traveling exhibition—The Quilts of Gee's Bend—when it moved from museum to museum across the country a few years before. I had marveled at the colors, the stitches, and most of all, the stories. These quilts and the women who made them are legendary. Born of necessity, stitched of practicality, the quilts were composed of whatever fabric was available—old scraps, a husband's overalls or plaid shirt, the stable parts cut and sewn in by hand. A scrap quilt, with bits of familiar fabric and careful stitches traveling through it, is a map of a life.

Fascinated by the history and in love with the quilts, I called a number I found online to ask about a visit. Maryann Pettway answered.

"Sure, hon, you can visit. When're you coming?"

"Do you need anything?" I asked. "Fabric? Sewing machines?"

"Well, yes," she replied, "sewing machines would be wonderful. Some of our ladies don't have their own. And fabric? We always love fabric!"

I drove the five-hour trip from New Orleans to Gee's Bend. Up with the dawn, I crossed the endless bridge over Lake Pontchartrain as pelicans swooped for breakfast. I wove through Mississippi's watery southern forests and into Alabama. Maryann had dictated the route, my notes on a scrap of paper on the seat beside me—my version of a map.

My heart jumped as road signs announced I was nearing Gee's Bend. Mileage signs dictated I slow down as I entered the town. Small homes, worn but well kept, dotted the landscape. I scanned the road ahead for signs showing where to find the quilters. After a few minutes, a sign announced, "You Are Now Leaving Gee's Bend." Wait, what? How did I miss it?

Turning back, I drove the road again, another short turn through town. I pulled over and called Maryann.

"I am here, but I can't find you."

"Honey, where are you?" Across the street from where I was parked, a woman on a cell phone opened her back door and walked down the steps. Maryann.

I stepped out of my car, stretching my legs after the long drive. We smiled at one another, and before I knew it, I was wrapped in a warm, soft hug.

"Did you have any trouble getting here?" she asked.

"Not until I got here!" I replied, laughing.

"Our building is right over there." She smiled, pointing up ahead on the right, and started walking.

"I'll pull my car in," I called after her. "I have your machines and fabric in the back." I spotted the long, narrow, hand-lettered sign announcing the building—another one that was easy to miss.

"Come on in," she said as I got out of the car. She beckoned me to follow her up the three short steps to the front door.

A long, white, wooden structure, the building was divided lengthwise to form two long rooms. Maryann led me into the room on the right. "This is where we work," she said. A woman sat at a frame to one side, carefully hand-stitching a quilt. She paused, looked up, and smiled, her needle raised.

"This is Chyna," Maryann said. Chyna carefully parked her needle in the quilt's surface. In a surprisingly deep voice, she welcomed me. Sliding a folding chair over, I sat down next to Chyna as she resumed her work, slow and even. The pace here was palpably slower, quieter than in other places. From the moment I walked through the door, my cadence shifted from the hum of the outside world to the steadiness of measured stitching.

Maryann invited me to follow her through the door at the end of the room and into the long left side. Folded and stacked quilts filled shelves along the walls.

"This is our store," Maryann explained, running her hands over the folded edges. "Lots of the ladies sell their quilts here."

"May I look at some?" I asked.

"Of course!" Maryann lifted a quilt off the shelf. Taking one end, I helped her unfold a study in blues and whites.

"I made this one," Maryann said proudly. "I call it Patience. Now, where is that piece? Oh, here! This is the smallest piece in the quilt." She pointed at a tiny triangle. "We don't throw anything away. We use everything. Using these tiny pieces is a challenge, but we love that!"

A map of a moment, the quilt, Patience, held a quiet power. Each piece had been thoughtfully placed, each tiny stitch adding to its whole. Running my hands over its soft edges, I folded back the corner to reveal the label, a piece of fabric hand-stitched in the corner with the quilt's name and the artist's written in pen. Maryann beamed with pride. I touched the tiniest piece before helping Maryann refold the quilt and place it back on the shelf.

"I have fabric for you," I said, "and machines. They are out in my car."

Together, we brought in five machines and two boxes of fabric, lining them up in the workroom. Maryann lifted out a piece of red and white cotton.

"Oh, I'm going to take this one!" she said. "The ladies will love this! And the machines—some of our quilters don't have their own machine. They have to come to the workroom to sew. Now they can sew at home too!" She looked up and smiled. "And maybe we can set up a classroom. We want to teach the children here what we know. So many of them leave as soon as they're old enough. There aren't so many jobs around here. If we don't teach them, our traditions will be lost."

"I can bring you some matching machines for your classroom next time I come," I offered, thinking of the refurbished machines we had recently received from the Bernina Corporation. We agreed on a plan for another delivery.

"Hey, anyone home?"

Maryann and I turned to see a man, followed by four women, stepping into the workroom. Maryann smiled.

"Margaret, I'd like you to meet our pastor. Pastor Joseph, this is Margaret. She just brought us some sewing machines."

"Praise the Lord!" Pastor Joseph beamed. An "Amen!" rose from the ladies behind him. "We just stopped by to say hello." Pastor Joseph and his flock had arrived in the church van parked outside.

"Chyna, how're you doing?" The pastor walked over to the quilt frame and sat down. "Mind if I take a few stitches?"

As his needle pierced the fabric, he began to hum, and the ladies joined in—a call to spontaneous praise.

"I'm gonna work so God can use me anywhere, Lord, anytime," the hymn began, first quiet, then filling the room as the women joined in harmony. I was silent, absolutely filled with the song. The room vibrated with roots far deeper than the floor I stood on, and I half expected the roof to open up to reveal the heavens. Pastor Joseph and the women, faces tipped skyward, sang with everything in them. I closed my eyes.

"I'm gonna live so God can use me anywhere, Lord, anytime," each verse built on the last. When the song was over, the walls continued vibrating.

"Can I get an 'Amen'?" the pastor shouted.

"Amen!" we all responded.

"Margaret, you keep on doing what you're doing. This is God's work." Pastor Joseph took my hand. "And ladies, you keep making these beautiful quilts. And friends, let's go out and help some folks in need. It's all God's work." With hugs and farewells, the pastor and his flock returned to the van outside.

As I hugged Maryann and Chyna goodbye, Maryann said, "Give me your address. I'm going to make something for you." I smiled and wrote it down. I didn't want to leave.

I followed the meandering thread of road guiding me back from Gee's Bend to New Orleans, my head and heart filled with the voices of the women, the resonance of the day. I drove for hours before I even turned on the radio.

A few months later, a package arrived at my home in Wisconsin. Hand-lettered, addressed to me, the return address was simply "M.P., Gee's Bend, AL." I carefully peeled open the padded envelope and reached inside, pulling out a little wall quilt—a map of tiny blue, yellow, black, and white pieces. I turned it over to reveal its name—*Kindness*.

Entering the church for a machine distribution, folks would lay eyes on a machine as if it were a long lost friend.

# Chapter 12

Each trip to New Orleans began about a month before departure, an inventory of waiting machines guiding my preparation. Seated at my desk at home or in a chair in Hans' makeshift classroom, I scanned the spreadsheet and began making phone calls.

The conversations would begin with a jog to the memory. "Hi, this is Margaret. Remember that day at Grace Church? The sewing machines? The line down the street?" At some point, the voice on the other end would say, "Oh yes!"

"Do you still need a machine?" I would ask, and the responses varied.

"Oh yes, I do!" or "I've already found a machine. You can pass mine along to someone else."

Sometimes the phone number would go nowhere, a void where a person had been. Sometimes I got a relative and gathered the information to track down the person on my list. When I finally reached my person, if I ever did, I gave them the information about the distribution date and the church's address. My finger moved down the list of names, my notes in columns reminding me of the results of each call. It was a long process, taking several sessions of calls—so many voices.

When at last I was in New Orleans and standing at the church flanked by sewing machines, people needed only to find me and give me their names. Tired faces gave way to excitement as we surveyed the machines.

"What kind of sewing do you do?" I'd ask. "What kind of machine did you have before?"

If someone on the list didn't show up, I would call them to see if they had forgotten, to make sure they were okay. In this spirit, I called Joan after her name remained unchecked on my list on a Saturday in 2008. Joan explained that she had been at work and couldn't get to the church in time. She apologized and asked if she could still have a machine.

"Of course," I said. "I've saved one for you. Let's set up a place to meet." We agreed to meet at the parking lot of a car parts store on busy Broad Street.

I waited in my car, eyes scanning the lot, a machine nested in the back. The city bus pulled up, and only one person stepped out, a woman with a tangle of long gray hair, shoulder stooped under the weight of a large tote bag. She squinted in the sunlight and looked around. I stepped out of my car.

"Joan?"

She smiled. "Yes? Margaret?"

Joan walked slowly toward my car. Her ankles were swollen.

"I have your machine right here," I said, opening the van's back door. I leaned in and eased the machine case to the back ledge of the cargo space. With a click of the latch, I lifted the lid, revealing a solid tan Kenmore. The vintage Kenmore is a workhorse of a machine, able to move effortlessly through layers of fabric or delicate silk. These machines purr, making the difficult seem easy.

"Oh," Joan murmured under her breath. She ran her hands over the machine, taking in its hand wheel, its curved bridge. "This is wonderful."

I pulled a second box toward the back. Lifting the flaps, I tugged at some folded cotton fabric. Red and white flowers, green vines, blue and white apron check.

"You are welcome to as much fabric as you'd like," I said. Joan's hands ran over the piece on top, a fine cottagey print. She took the pieces out, one by one, and held them up to her face, inhaling.

"I learned to sew when I was a little girl," Joan began, the red and white floral fabric soft in her hands. "I loved it. It was always an escape for me." She continued, "We didn't have much money, certainly no money for new fabric. My mom sometimes burned cigarette holes in her clothes—she would give them to me. I would cut out the burned parts and sew with what was left." Joan picked up a piece of blue and white checked fabric. "I haven't had a machine in so long. And new fabric," her voice trailed off. She raised her eyes to meet mine, a window into her reality.

Packing her tote bag with brightly printed fabric and securely clicking the machine's cover, we worked side by side to prepare her for the trip home. I walked her to the bus stop, carrying her machine as the bus pulled up.

"I'm going home to sew," Joan said, smiling as the bus door folded open with a metallic squeak. She hoisted the machine up the steps, and I watched from the curb as Joan navigated the aisle and found a seat. She looked out of the cloudy window and waved. I raised my hand goodbye. She turned and looked straight ahead as the bus pulled away.

I sat longer than I'd expected on the back bumper of the car, feeling Joan's exhaustion, riding the waves of her joy in receiving a machine. In that moment of reflection, as I continue to be, I was reminded that doing this work, if one can even call it that, is an answer to an invitation that continues to arrive, one that comes from far beyond myself. I have been reminded, again and again, that I must let my heart lead the way and trust it knows where to go. This idea, arriving so naturally, has permeated every fiber of who I am.

In preparation for my next trip to New Orleans, my finger again ran down the list. When I called a woman named Anna and went through the familiar script, "Remember the day at the church? The sewing machines? The line down the street?"

Anna replied, "Oh yes!"

"Do you still need one?" I asked.

"I sure do," Anna's voice held a smile. "My fiancé and I bought an old house in Central City—it used to be a drug house." She went on, "We are making it into a community center. You see, folks in this neighborhood are afraid. Afraid to come out of their homes, afraid to let their children play outside. We want to create a safe space for people to gather, a place where kids can come after school, a community center." Anna continued, "So we are renovating this old house. You should see it. It's looking really good." Anna's pride spilled through the phone. "We'd like to offer classes too," she said, "like sewing classes. That's why we need the machine. In fact, do you think we could have three machines?" her voice was hopeful.

"I think we can make that happen," I said, as her idea of building community stirred within me.

We made arrangements and finished our call. Within minutes, my phone sounded. Anna's voice, now familiar, lit the line.

"You know, I was wondering, do you think we could have five machines?" Anna asked hopefully.

"Sure," I said. "We will make it work."

Tucking my phone in my pocket, I headed to the back of the store, into the warehouse. I flipped a switch, and the dim bulb on the high ceiling flickered on. The ready machines were lined up on the wooden shelves. I ran my hand over the smooth metal edges, the familiar colors and sizes revealing each machine's capabilities. Hoping to identify five that would work together in a classroom, I searched for similar models, threading patterns, and bobbin placement. Sighing, I stepped back and addressed the lineup.

"Show me," I whispered, my words rising with the dust specks that filled the space.

Not finding even two that were compatible, I shook my head and headed back onto the sales floor. Why had I promised five machines without taking a look first?

"Later," my words slipped out in a whisper.

I had an appointment to keep and needed to leave the store for a few hours. I anxiously made my way across town to the Wisconsin Public Television studios on University Avenue in Madison. I was going to meet Nancy Zieman for the very first time. Her encouragement during our few phone conversations was motivating.

"This is important work," she said when she invited me to film a "Nancy's Corner" segment. "Nancy's Corner" filled five minutes at the end of each episode of her successful sewing program, *Sewing With Nancy*. Nancy's straightforward, concise direction had helped sewers for years. Adding "Nancy's Corner" gave Nancy a chance to interview people who were giving back and building community, an impulse that came naturally to Nancy. I was honored to be invited.

Entering Nancy Zieman's studio felt new and familiar all at once. I had watched her so often, her on-air sewing studio warm and familiar. Nancy's assistant led me to my chair for the taping where Nancy was waiting.

"How are you?" she asked, as though we'd known each other forever.

"Nervous," I replied.

She smiled. "You know, I'm a little nervous each time we tape one of these, and I've been doing it for so long!" Her ease calmed me.

"We'll just tape it, and if we have to do it over, we can," she reassured me.

The camera started rolling, and Nancy recited her introduction. We fell into it as two old friends. Nancy asked about how The Sewing Machine Project began, and I smiled nervously as I described the idea's "arrival" and the notion of guiding it on its path. Nancy understood the depth of meaning, her deep faith shining through as she nodded. Soon, our five minutes were up.

"Well, what do you think?" she said. "Do you want to use that one, or should we do it again?"

"I think it's just fine."

"So do I," she said. We hugged goodbye, and she was off to another set, preparing a sewing demonstration. I hovered in the dark studio space for a minute, soaking it all in. *I was in Nancy's studio!*

When I returned to the store, I entered through the front door, the cowbell announcing my arrival. Just inside the door were five sewing machines. Lined up, exactly alike, threaded with shining Gütermann thread, the machines waited. I stopped, puzzled.

"Rebecca," I called to my workmate, "what's the deal with these machines?"

Rebecca walked over to greet me. "While you were gone, a lady stopped in. She is a sewing teacher but has downsized her classroom. She had five extra machines. These are for you. She wanted you to know they are classroom grade, identical, well maintained, and have just been tuned up."

I was given what I needed.

When I drove to New Orleans a month later, the five machines sat snugly in the back of the fourteen-foot rental truck. These big vehicles, at first daunting, had become comfortable. The bounce of the seats, the simplicity of the dashboard, and the feeling of commandeering something with so much length, width, and height were now familiar. As I drove the truck slowly down the narrow street, my eyes searched for Anna's place. Seeing it, I veered to the curb to park and immediately felt a jolt, heard a crunch, and came to an abrupt stop. *Oh no.* I opened the door and lowered myself down the truck's steps to see what was going on. The top of the box was lodged on the swooping branch of an oak tree, those whose lively bodies grace so many city streets. I'd driven right into it. My heart sank as I saw the hole the tree had made in a truck that wasn't mine. *This was going to be expensive.*

I looked around and saw a woman I could only assume was Anna stepping out of a building on the corner.

"Anna?" I called.

"Hi!" she said, smiling as she approached the truck.

"Yikes! What happened?" her eyes focused on the top of the truck and the tree, now joined above our heads.

"I have your machines in the back. Wait ⊠til I tell you the story of

93

how they came to be!" I said. The truck and the tree weren't going anywhere, so I moved into full-on delivery mode.

Anna and I unloaded the five sewing machines and carried them inside. She had tables ready—new homes for the machines in her makeshift sewing space.

"Let me give you a tour!" she said excitedly. We moved through the house-turned-community center as she shared the thoughtful improvements they had made with an eye toward service. "This is where kids can come after school," she said. "See, we have snacks ready for them." Leading me to the main room, Anna explained that neighbors would be welcome to hold weddings, community meals, funerals—events marking the moments of lives—in this new space. Her enthusiasm was contagious.

When we finally said goodbye, I returned to the reality of the truck, still hanging up on the tree branch outside. I turned the key and slowly backed up. Miraculously, the truck let go of the branch, or perhaps the branch let go of the truck. I opened the door and stood on the seat to get a closer look. There was indeed a hole in the top of the truck. I fished in the glove compartment for the paperwork. *Please let this be covered!* My finger ran down the page. I'd purchased insurance, but it specifically stated that the top of the truck wasn't covered. *Ugh.* I decided to drive straight to the local Budget truck rental center to fess up.

Pulling up to the rental agency, I took a deep breath and headed inside. "Hi, I rented a truck in Wisconsin to bring sewing machines here to New Orleans. Just this morning, I was parking the truck and ran into a tree branch." The rental agent, a young man with a kind smile, raised his eyebrows, and we walked outside together.

"Hmm, well, I haven't seen this problem before," he said. "I'm not even sure what paperwork we should be filling out!"

"I did purchase insurance," I offered. "I'm hoping it covers something like this. And I'm done delivering sewing machines, so if I could leave the truck here, that would be great. I will be renting a smaller vehicle for the remainder of my visit." *One*, I thought, *that sits lower than the tree branches!*

"You can certainly return it," he said, "but I honestly don't know how they will deal with this. How about if you leave your number, and I'll have someone contact you."

I gladly handed over the keys to the truck. Stepping outside, I took some photos of the hole, just in case, and hollered goodbye.

I never heard another word.

The ladies of the Antigona NGO were wowed with the automatic buttonhole feature of the sewing machine we delivered.

# Chapter 13

"Welcome to Pristina," our host greeted us warmly. My eyes scanned the hotel lobby as Gani stepped in, continuing the conversation in Albanian.

He turned to us. "They'll need your passports."

"Po, po," Gani said, turning back to the man behind the desk. "Yes, yes."

I looked into the desk clerk's face, the lines a map I didn't recognize. Behind him, the wall was filled with photos—stern-faced family watching us as we dug in our bags and produced identification. Gani's exchange with the man was fast and punctuated, unfamiliar letters and syllables rising and falling. One by one, we presented our passports. The desk clerk's eyes shifted from passport to face, regarding each of us sternly. He carefully stacked our documents and turned toward the closet behind him.

"May I have my passport back?" I asked nervously.

"No," Gani replied. "They'll keep them behind the desk while you're here. Don't worry."

Pristina, Kosovo, was a whole new landscape, everything new and different and admittedly a bit scary, especially through flight-weary eyes. Once again, I was invited into the unknown. Once again, I was answering through trust.

We were each given a room key, and I gathered my luggage. Heading for the darkened stairway, I looked back over my shoulder as our host locked the closet door, our passports inside. I'd just arrived in Kosovo and already was imagining being stranded there forever, a captive of the guy behind the desk.

Al, John, Gani, and I flew from Chicago to Kosovo on a variety of missions. This was Gani's country. A native Kosovar, Gani came to the U.S. during the war in the 1990s and opened a tidy family restaurant in Monona in a strip mall that Al owned. Over the years, Al had gotten to know Gani and his family. He had listened and learned about the immense hardship Gani's community and country had seen as a result of war. Over the years, as their friendship bloomed, Gani and Al began to discuss sustainable ways to help Kosovo's recovery effort. Gani remained deeply connected with his friends, Fadil and Raba, active citizens in Skenderaj, Gani's home village. Caring deeply for their community, Gani, Fadil, and Raba were finding creative ways to be of service, to help their country move forward.

In addition to working in loans full time at the local bank, Raba had helped to found Antigona, an NGO (non-governmental organization) featuring a vibrant sewing workshop. Employing five women in 2009, Antigona did a strong business in custom women's apparel.

The dream of the women of Antigona was to expand the workshop to offer sewing education, producing graduates who could potentially find jobs in the region. This work would make a critical difference to war widows searching for a means to support their families. In their region alone, the war had left over nine hundred widows, each coping with grief and loss of income at the same time.

Al was my neighbor. He had arrived on my back porch on an unseasonably warm March evening earlier in 2009, curious to know more about the work I was doing, about the sewing machines I collected and delivered. I invited Al in, and we stood in the quiet of my kitchen. I told him about collecting and delivering sewing machines first to India and Sri Lanka and about the many trips to New Orleans.

"I have a friend I'd like you to meet. His name is Gani. We'd like to talk to you about getting machines over to Kosovo." The excitement in Al's voice hinted at a plan unfolding in his head. We agreed on a meeting date, as I made a mental reminder to check the map and see exactly where Kosovo was!

A week later, Gani, Al, and I sat around my dining room table, sipping spiced tea, warming our bones as March's more seasonable cold seeped through the walls. Gani described Skenderaj, and Antigona, his voice staccato with enthusiasm.

"I'd like to send some sewing machines to the ladies in Kosovo. Antigona would like to expand its business and teach more ladies to sew. I am thinking they could make uniforms. With more people, they could take on more contracts."

I listened carefully to Gani's big idea, quietly wondering how and if this could unfold. I remembered the faces of those who listened to my big idea of a charity given to sharing sewing machines only a few years before, their expressions warm and open. It was now my turn to extend that openness to Gani. I smiled.

"What do you need?" I asked.

One month later, Gani and I loaded twenty sewing machines into the back of a van he had borrowed from a friend. I had reached out to Bernina of America, sharing the story of Antigona, and they responded immediately with a donation. The machines landed in my dining room around the very table where we made our plan.

In a dark, drafty warehouse in Chicago, Gani and I loaded the machines into a room-sized container, nudging them into the last remaining spaces. I gazed into the shadows, marveling at the immense load. Medical supplies, clothing, shoes, a car! The forty-foot container was set to travel to Kosovo in the upcoming days. We added our treasures just under the wire.

I walked into Gani's restaurant a few days later to meet Al and tell him about the delivery. The cheery restaurant buzzed with energy. I found a table by the window, and Al sat across from me.

"Did you get everything loaded?" he asked. My enthusiasm matched his as I described the newness of each step. Al's face lit up as he recognized my delight in the process.

"You know Gani and I are going to Kosovo in June," Al said. We'll be able to check on Antigona and see how they're doing with the machines."

I couldn't begin to imagine the landscape of Kosovo. What was it like? The people? The sounds? The smells?

A rare courage rose in my voice, catching me by surprise.

"Really? Wow! Do you think I might be able to go along?" My words were solid.

"I think we could arrange that," Al said. "After all, you pulled this sewing machine donation together, and we're really grateful. I'd be happy to bring you along and take care of your expenses."

Al went on to say that besides himself and Gani, a third man would be joining the team. John was a large-scale Wisconsin farmer who had worked with USAID and the University of Wisconsin on farming development. He was coming along to take a look at the existing farms around Skenderaj to help develop a plan to create more sustainable farming. Not knowing many farmers, I immediately created a mental image of a big old guy in a feed cap and overalls.

Early on a Saturday morning in June 2009, Al's car pulled into the driveway, ready to travel to Chicago's O'Hare Airport. Propelled by curiosity and excitement, I asked for their help as I hefted my suitcase and two sewing machines into the trunk. I was carrying a fancy Baby Lock with embroidery and an overlock machine. We loaded the trunk, and I hopped in the back seat next to John. He was nothing like the picture in my head. Dressed in a business suit, fit and handsome, he smiled and extended his hand.

"Hi there, I'm Margaret," I said as I shook his hand.

We flew from O'Hare to JFK and from JFK to Pristina, Kosovo. Upon arrival at JFK, we searched for the Kosova Airlines desk. A new airline, Kosova, had only begun offering flights one week before. The airline was clearly a source of pride for Gani, another sign of the rebuilding of his beloved country. Airline restrictions dictated that we collect and recheck our luggage at JFK. My suitcase and sewing machines circled on the luggage belt, and I loaded them on our cart. We rechecked our luggage and waited for our late-night flight at the Kosova Air gate.

After quite a delay, our night growing longer, we boarded the plane. The previous Air China logo peeked through the thin paint as we took our seats in the front row. John and I sat next to each other, easy conversation flowing about family, jobs, and our missions in Kosovo.

"You know," he said, "you're nothing like I imagined you'd be."

"Neither are you," I replied. "I imagined you a big old farmer in overalls and a feed cap," I said, laughing.

"And I imagined you as an old gray-haired lady carrying her sewing bag," he said. We laughed at the stereotypes we'd adopted and the ease with which we let them go. Our friendship was sealed.

In the quiet moments of the long flight, I could feel the distance growing between my life at home and a new territory I'd yet to discover. I reflected on the things I'd put on hold with my departure. Walt and I were struggling. We had been for a few years, and we both recognized it. Separation is never one big event but rather a million tiny pinpricks, and there had been many. Two years before, I'd begun to wonder whether it would be better to make my way on my own. I slowly realized I had been operating on autopilot, following the dictates of what "should" come next in life without listening to what my heart was saying. In quiet moments, I'd slip into the pantry to hide the tears that seemingly sprang out of nowhere. But they weren't out of nowhere. Frustrated and feeling alone, I would imagine what my world might look like if we were apart, and that world was out of focus. Try as I might, I couldn't make it come into view. He and I would try talking through things, recognizing our struggle, and seeing that we were coming from completely different places.

My internal voice began to speak up, reminding me that this wasn't the first time I'd considered a path I could not see. Walt and I were both growing. His new career in facilitation filled him with passion and drive and a new public exposure he loved. My growth was internal. The pulse that The Sewing Machine Project created within me imparted a new sense of purpose, a new belief in myself that had never existed before. We were operating side by side but no longer together.

"We need some counseling," I said, "or we're not going to be able to manage this."

"That, or we just decide we're headed in two directions and let go of one another," he'd replied.

I let the questions course through my veins, wondering how I would support myself and feel being single in a community of couples. My children, Alec in college and Maddie finishing high school, would undoubtedly be affected. Where would I find the bandwidth to support their needs when I wasn't even sure how I'd manage my own? I waited for the answers to arrive, for a clear path through the darkness, but nothing came.

Finally, one evening, I walked in the dark around our familiar neighborhood, a path I could practically navigate with my eyes closed. Suddenly, I was filled with a new sense of peace as I envisioned myself spinning in the dark, hands toward the sky. I was settling into myself, and though I didn't have the answers, I knew I'd be okay. I trusted a path I could not yet see.

We ended up deciding to divorce, and the court date loomed shortly after my return from Kosovo.

In the quiet dark of the airplane, I cried. The day-to-day of my life was a distraction, with kids, appointments, and life's busyness. There was nothing to do in the airplane, and the reality of our decision flooded me. I'd known Walt since tenth grade. He was my best friend.

The decision traveled with me like additional luggage.

We arrived in Pristina midmorning the next day. I kept an eye on Gani as we moved from the relative familiarity of an airplane to the new world of the airport. The language spoken around me, Albanian, was one I'd never heard. The air smelled of sweat and spice. Gani led us to the baggage claim area, a holding space with suitcases lined up and stacked on the tile floor. I saw the sewing machines first, then my suitcase, and nudged each piece out of the lineup.

The customs official eyed the sewing machines packed in their original boxes and addressed me in fast Albanian. I looked to Gani for a translation, and he stepped in. An animated conversation followed, voices rising and falling in a dramatic staccato, and an agreement was transacted. Finally, Gani looked at me and said, "It's okay. Now we go." We walked through the turnstile and out the exit door, stepping into the humid blast. We were greeted instantly by Gani's uncle, waiting outside the door. Our luggage and machines crammed in the trunk, we began the bumpy, dusty journey into town.

My eyes were fixed out the window. Everything was new—the golden dry landscape, the road changing from rough pavement to dirt, people cooking in market stalls, steam rising from kettles on fires and tiny electric stoves. I couldn't stop looking.

Swerving through Pristina's busy, narrow streets, our car eventually slowed as we drove up a narrow alley and abruptly stopped. Gani opened the door and stepped out, saying, "We're here."

We arrived at our hotel, our home for the duration of the visit, for a brief stop before continuing to Skenderaj. We checked in and surrendered our passports. Gani translated the directions to my room, instructing me to drop off my bag and meet back in the lobby in fifteen minutes. I dragged my suitcase, bumping up the stairs and down the darkened hallway, feeling the weight of the long night. I fit the key in the lock and opened the door. A small tidy room met me, sunlight filtering through the window's gold-flowered curtains. Leaving my suitcase by the door, I stood in the center of the room, eyes closed, allowing the reality of where I was to sink in. I crossed the room to look out the window onto the courtyard below. Shaded and quiet, the garden, with its few tables, looked like a lovely place to relax. I dug through my suitcase and found my toiletry kit, taking out face wash and my toothbrush. The bathroom was tiny but had everything I needed—a tiled shower and a miniature sink. I regarded my wavy reflection in the mirror. A tired face looked back. I unwrapped the soap and sudsed up my face and neck, the floral scent filling my nose, and took a little "bird bath," as my mother would say.

When I returned, Gani, Al, and John were waiting in the lobby at the bottom of the stairs. Smiling, I joined the group, the earlier qualms of unfamiliarity long since gone as we headed back into the city's bathwater heat. It was time to meet Gani's family and friends in Skenderaj.

The car bumped and lurched on the uneven streets as we drove through town. Just outside Pristina, the paved road ended with a bump, a noticeable drop to the pitted surface below. The war had left the roads peppered with deep potholes that seemed to attract the car at every turn. Gani explained that the country has just begun to address infrastructure, and the roads were next on the agenda. Dust swirled around and in the car. I sat in the back seat, wedged between Al and John, while Gani and his uncle caught up in the front in a flood of fast Albanian. I stretched to look past my companions and out the window. Dusty and dry, yet beautiful in its starkness, with little farms dotting the hillsides, the landscape looked golden. Skenderaj was a half hour away. Gani's face softened in recognition as we pulled into his village's town square, full of activity, welcoming us. We got out of the car and stretched our legs, the long journey making its presence known in every muscle, every bone.

People poured off of a little terrace on the town square—Gani's friends, waiting for our arrival. Raba was among the first to meet us. She took my arm.

Sensing my unease, she said, "You will meet my daughter tomorrow. She can translate for you during your stay." I smiled, sinking into her kindness. We followed the others to a friendly terrace, where a table and unmatched chairs awaited us. It felt so good to sit down. Raba pulled up a chair next to me.

Little groups of friends stood together in the square, talking and gesturing as they connected in an intimacy that was new to me, catching up with one another. I sipped a lemon soda, its icy tartness falling across my tongue.

"*Faleminderit*," thank you. A tall, handsome gentleman approached our table, and Gani's face lit up. He rose and hugged the man tightly. Turning and smiling, he said, "This is Fadil." Fadil sat beside Raba, the intimacy between husband and wife immediately apparent as their heads dipped together in quiet conversation. The waiter slid more chairs around our table as our crowd grew, friends stopping to greet Gani and welcome him home. Our group had become a party, a tangle of names I found hard to understand, much less pronounce.

By the time we walked across the square for dinner, our group had grown from seven to twenty. The waiter met us at the door, hugging Gani, and led us to a long table in the back of the restaurant. Plates of cheeses, baskets of bread, warm tasty burek, meaty kebabs, and meat pies dotted the table. Marinated salads of greens and cucumbers, vinegary and tart, spicy and sweet, arrived. The food kept coming, punctuated by cigarette breaks and wine. I sat back in my chair and listened to this language, so foreign to me, moving like music. The meal lasted three hours, and I delighted in watching Gani's delight as he reunited with his family and friends.

Raba introduced me to Flora, the woman who ran Antigona's sewing room, making the sewing connection all the more real.

After dinner, we walked back to the car, Raba and Flora linking their arms with mine. Their warmth and kindness, and my long day, caused a stir of emotion in me. Over ten years later, I can still remember how it felt when they embraced me.

"We'll see you again tomorrow," they said.

I nodded sleepily. "Yes, I'll see you in the morning."

Back in my hotel room that night, I looked in the mirror. A very long day was behind me.

"I am me," I said aloud. This phrase first escaped my lips when I traveled alone in Greece in 1985. I'd had the sense of being in my skin somehow, of recognizing my life, as if standing outside of myself and looking in, seeing the coming and going of thoughts, understanding for the first time that I was a soul inhabiting a body, inhabiting a life. "I am me," I would say to myself as the waters of the Mediterranean cooled my feet. *I am me*, I would think, when I stood before the stone once inhabited by the Oracle of Delphi. "I am me," I would whisper as I drank retsina in the company of a band of wild Greeks in a bar in Athens, watching the men dance, handkerchiefs held high.

"I am me."

Standing alone in my shadowy cozy room, I looked in the mirror, letting the journey fill me. I was in Kosovo, on a mission to deliver sewing machines, because of an idea that was, and yet wasn't, mine. "I am me."

Sliding into bed, I let the silence, the breadth of the day's emotions, flood through me. The joy of the journey, the sadness of the divorce, and the trust in the unknown swirled as I drifted off to sleep. That night I dreamed I awoke in a little rowboat in the middle of a lake, with no land in sight. I was alone, and in dream language, I knew I'd been tethered to a pier when I'd fallen asleep at the bottom of the boat. Waking in the dream, my dreaming self realized that the knot holding me to the pier, to the known, had been quietly untied, and I'd drifted. The calm of the water reflected the calm within me as I looked in every direction. I felt no worry, trusting that I would be okay.

The next day, we traveled the dusty, bumpy road back to Skenderaj. I was so curious to see what the Antigona sewing room looked like, excited to meet the women, and grateful to have a translator. Raba's daughter, Fjolle, would be my companion.

Right on schedule, Fjolle was waiting when we pulled into Skenderaj's town square. Sixteen years old, with shiny brown hair and a mischievous smile, Fjolle greeted me warmly. In perfect English, she welcomed me and gave me the lowdown on the day.

"We'll go visit the ladies for awhile," she said, "and then meet Gani, Al, and John for lunch." With that, we said our goodbyes to the men, and I was in her hands.

We didn't need to walk far. Antigona inhabited a room on the second floor of one of the buildings on the square. An old office building or perhaps a government building, the war had taken its toll. Broken windows, dripping water, and trash swirling around our feet into piles in the corners, we walked through the shadowy concrete hallways and up the steps to the second floor. Turning a corner, we heard voices. Fjolle opened a door, and the light of the faces within greeted us.

Flora met us, taking my arm and introducing me to the ladies one by one, Shefkije, Qefsere, Ajshe, and Selvete. These women, working on Juki industrial sewing machines donated years before from the

U.K., were pros. Shefkjie worked on a free motion machine, focused and steady, stitching intricate golden embroidery designs freehand at top speed. I squinted, expecting to see the design she followed, but there was none. The free-motion machines I was familiar with used a laser to guide the sewer along the design. For Shefkjie, the intricate curls and swirls moved directly from her head through her fingers.

Ajshe sat near the back, working on an industrial serger. She finished seams with skill, precision, and speed, moving from one piece to the next. Flora stood at the central work table. As the matron of the sewing room, Flora worked with her clients, determining their needs and designing custom clothing, then handing the assignments off to her artisans. Lining one side wall were mannequins, displaying some of their recent creations, evening gowns and blazers.

"Who buys these gowns?" I asked Fjolle. The sparkling luxury was in strong contrast to our dilapidated surroundings. Flora explained that there were still women with money who had all their custom clothes made.

Other than the sewing room, the complex was empty. Hearing voices, we turned to see Gani and Al coming up the stairs, carrying the Baby Lock machine and the overlocker we had hauled from Wisconsin. The ladies gathered around and were introduced to Al. Excited to unload and explore the machines with the ladies, I quickly took the Baby Lock from Gani, setting the box on the floor. Piece by piece, we unloaded the machine and its embroidery components. I had imagined this moment. I couldn't wait to show the sewers the decorative stitches, the embroidery functions—all of the bells and whistles of this complicated machine.

Once we were set up, the ladies took over. We all admired the fancy Baby Lock and its straight, zigzag, and alphabet stitching. They needed little guidance. We took out the automatic buttonhole foot. This type of function is pretty standard on household sewing machines available in the U.S., making the creation of a buttonhole surprisingly simple. All that is necessary is to insert the chosen button in the buttonhole foot, and the machine does the rest, stitching out a perfectly sized buttonhole. These ladies had never seen anything like this. With all of the features of this complicated machine, the buttonhole function was the one that captured them. One button after another, we stitched perfect buttonholes, the ladies smiling with delight at their success.

We spent the entire afternoon getting to know one another, Fjolle offering skilled translation back and forth. Our languages were so foreign, but there was no denying the common language of sewing.

In the evening, Al and I sat and talked over dinner.

"Al, the ladies say they would like to open their own storefront. You know, a place where they can showcase ready-to-wear garments and greet their clients in a more professional setting."

Al listened thoughtfully. A businessman at heart, a businessman *with* heart, Al led with careful consideration in a spirit of kindness and generosity.

"Maybe we should visit some sites and see what it would cost to rent a space."

"Actually, Al, the ladies have already researched some locations. There is a little space in the Skenderaj marketplace that would be perfect. I have the numbers they shared with me if you would like to see them."

We were back in the car early the next morning, headed to Skenderaj and the Antigona sewing room. The ladies were already hard at work when we arrived. With Fjolle translating, Al shared his vision.

"I would be happy to give you the money for the first six months' rent. I will finance the purchase of fabric and supplies for you to create a line of ready-to-wear garments," Al announced.

Light filled the room and the faces of each woman as they listened. They talked amongst themselves, with Flora speaking for the group.

"Al, you have given us such a gift. We will make you proud."

The room crackled with energy as the ladies began sharing ideas and plans.

After lunch, we all walked together to visit the space in the marketplace where Flora envisioned the shop. The tiny storefront left a lot to the imagination, but Flora was undaunted. She carefully walked around the room, sharing her vision of the layout, where mannequins would stand, and where work would be done. Through her eyes, I could see the future of her business.

Flora and Raba arrived in Pristina the next day, meeting Al, Gani, and me. We traveled together to a fabric distributor, a dark warehouse in the hills over Pristina. Metal shelves towered, piled high with bolts of fabric—silks, fine cottons, some wools. I ran my hands over the textures and fibers, happily surprised at the resources available in this recovering country.

A young man was our guide. Walking along with him, Flora moved slowly and carefully, her hand running over the various weaves as she envisioned the possibilities. She stopped and pointed at a bolt, and the young man carried it to the door, letting her see the color and fiber in natural light.

As she chose bolts of fabric, the young man whisked them away to the cutting table. I wandered off down other aisles. The rough weave of the silks, the softness of the wool, and the slippery taffeta were braille to my fingers.

Three hours later, we loaded piles of folded fabric into the back of Gani's car. The garments that would rise from this cloth were already constructed in Flora's imagination. She was gifted at listening and interpreting a design, transforming it into a paper pattern and then to fabric, allowing it to melt over the form as she studied its drape and movement.

John and I sat in the hotel garden that evening, sharing our day. John had been out that day looking at area farms, inspecting the cows, and noting their feed and medications. Excitedly, I told him about our visit to the fabric warehouse. We clinked our bottles of Peja beer together, toasting the passion each of us held for our work.

The following day, Fjolle met me upon our arrival in Skenderaj and led me to their home, just off the main street. Raba had invited me for tea. We entered the concrete structure through the back, walking up a few flights of the open stairwell to reach her family's apartment. Small and tidy, love and family were at the forefront as I scanned the family photos and heirloom stitched samplers that dotted the walls. The weather was warm, and Raba suggested we go outside on the balcony to enjoy the occasional breeze. The three of us sat on the ground, shoulder to shoulder, hip to hip, our knees scrunched up and toes meeting in the middle, cradling cups of spicy tea. We pored over family photo albums, Raba proudly explaining who was who with Fjolle translating.

Two weeks later, I stepped onto the plane, at once ready to go home and wistful in the leaving. We had delivered sewing machines and made a plan with Flora and her team to move forward with their design house. But the visit went far deeper than this. I had walked through the streets of a village that had seen unimaginable sorrow, my arms linked with those of strong, resilient women. I was welcomed into a culture that had previously been a point on a map and discovered a country with its own set of loves and loyalties. I worked side by side with new friends in an effort to make life better for the people we met. I had stepped beyond the uneasiness, again and again, trusting I would find my way.

I leaned against the airplane window, taking one last look before takeoff. I was heading into a changing life at home and wasn't sure what was ahead.

"I am me," I whispered.

The world that awaited me when I returned from Kosovo was changing beneath my feet as I was once again invited into the unknown. And though I could not predict what was to come, I trusted with all my heart that I could navigate it, that somehow, my little boat would eventually find the shore.

Three weeks after arriving home, Walt and I met at the county courthouse for our divorce hearing. We'd agreed to a collaborative divorce—no animosity, no cruelty. It simply was. When the hearing was over, we walked to a local brewpub and had a beer. It seemed the same as ever, yet everything had changed.

"I want you to know," Walt said, "that I will never disparage you."

I smiled. "You know I'll always love you."

He gave me a serious look. "And I'm grateful for how you stayed home and raised our kids while I built my career. It's your turn now. I will support you. I'll pay your bills. You go out and save the world."

I looked at him in disbelief. "Seriously?" I asked.

"Yes," he said.

And he did.

Walt supported me in many ways. I felt the impact of his financial support every day. Walt assisted with our organizational strategic planning, and helped us develop an inventory system—surveys and metrics to chart our growth. He was gifted in organizational thinking and shared his gifts with me and the organization I'd founded.

We met every so often for dinner, talking over the places where our lives intersected—the house, kids. We talked about struggles and triumphs, new and old. Laughing over sandwiches at a bar, we were often asked, "How long have you two been married?" We'd smile at each other and then at the bartender. "That's just it; we're divorced."

MARGARET JOHN JANKOWSKI

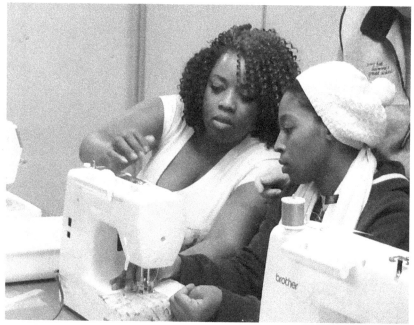

Students learn sewing and machine care in our local classes, but it is the community that is created that truly shines.

# Chapter 14

"**H**ere, hon, like this."

Trish cradled Deki's hands, gently curving her fingers through the scissors handle. Moving the blades, *shhh shhh*, in and out, their hands intertwined, Deki became accustomed to the exercise. She beamed.

"Now, try cutting," Trish said, positioning the sky-blue dotted calico between the blades. Deki's delighted laugh over the *shhh shhh* of the blades was music.

Around the table sat ten Bhutanese women and men in a sunny upstairs classroom at the Catholic Multicultural Center in Madison. Steffani Lincecum, an SMP board member and accomplished seamstress, had volunteered to lead the class. Drawing clear pictograms on the whiteboard, Steffani conveyed the lesson. Dechen, our translator, explained the details, the finer points, deftly moving between English and Bhutanese.

Establishing a local presence in Madison had been a journey. Bob Heideman, a charter board member and retired educator, was adamant. Bob and I met at one of my earliest presentations about gathering sewing machines. After the meeting, he made his way to me, introducing himself. "I think what you're doing is wonderful," he said. Smart, world-conscious, and interested, Bob was always eager to learn. He was brimming with ideas when he joined The Sewing Machine Project board in 2007.

"Margaret, it's fine to send machines to other countries and other states, but you also need to pay attention here at home." Bob's words stuck.

Discerning what the local effort would look like and what would be useful and possible took a while. We had begun with a sewing machine lending library. A set of Bernette machines, a gift from Bernina International in Steckborn, Switzerland, formed the library's core. Twenty similar machines were made available to groups within Dane County for use in short-term sewing courses. I contacted community leaders and educators, raising awareness around this resource. Though we had a few interested groups, most backed away when they realized we were offering the tools without the teacher. The idea didn't take hold.

A short paragraph in a church bulletin caught my eye: "Furniture needed for newly arrived Bhutanese refugees setting up apartments in Madison." I tucked the bulletin in my bag, questions rising in my mind. What was it like to be moved from your home (your life!) to a refugee camp and then to Madison? What was it like to navigate a system so different from what you knew? The schools, the buses, the grocery store so big, with different and strange products, a new language. I called the number listed in the article.

"Hi, my name is Margaret," I began, explaining our work. "Do you think our new Bhutanese arrivals would like sewing machines?"

The tiny Bhutanese community met monthly at the Catholic Multicultural Center on Beld Street in Madison. When asked at the meeting about sewing machines, thirty people—more than half of the group—were interested.

"But we'll need a teacher," I was told. "A few people used machines in the refugee camp, but most only know hand sewing and have never worked on a sewing machine."

Steffani agreed to teach, and we piloted a beginner class the following month. The bright little meeting room on the second floor hummed with students, our volunteers, and students' sponsors—Lutheran Social Services volunteers who "adopted" families as they arrived in the city.

Steffani's grace and patience radiated as she carefully taught each step. Everything was new, from how to insert pins to how to hold scissors. The students caught on quickly, their enthusiasm contagious as they revved their machines.

"*Bistari*," Steffani said. "Slowly."

Each week, the students arrived early, eager to begin. Women leaned into one another as they learned together. The topics of their conversations, I realized, extended far beyond sewing. Daily concerns, problem-solving, and the words of friendship rose in the hum of the sewing room. Isolated by language and unsure in a new culture, our students often felt alone in their day-to-day lives. In the sewing room, they learned a skill while finding community and friendship. Forming bonds with their Bhutanese peers and new friendships with the volunteer helpers, the lessons in the sewing room pushed beyond the threading of machines, pressing through cultural walls. A broader community arose.

The women proudly displayed their work at the end of the six-week session: a wallet, an apron, a simple pair of child's pants.

"You have done a great job," I said, waiting for the translator to convey the compliment. "Now your machine is your own. It's time to take it home. It's yours."

Carefully packing the machines and adding scissors, thread, and fabric as the last class ended, we couldn't believe our six weeks were already over. Steffani and her students, our volunteers, sponsors, and the center staff bowed to one another.

"Namaste."

The students, brimming with creative possibility, asked about more classes.

"We want to learn to make clothes for ourselves, our children!" they said, and Steffani graciously agreed. Teaching all of the interested beginners and enthusiastic advanced students, we offered classes until everyone who had expressed interest had a machine and the confidence to use it. When we considered how they might pay it forward, the answer came easily. Students who had completed the beginner class returned to mentor the new beginners as guides and translators. These students, who had once entered the room timid and unsure, sat confidently with the new students, sharing what they'd learned.

Week by week, session by session, we made our way through the list of interested Bhutanese clients. The center became a familiar place with a rhythm all its own. I wondered what might come next. How could we continue this momentum? The answer was there, waiting in a call from the center director.

"Other center clients are interested in learning to sew. Would you be willing to offer more classes?"

Steffani's hands were full with a successful book contract, so Rebecca Sites stepped in. Rebecca, a talented local costumer, worked with theater groups, taught kids' classes, and had a bespoke sewing business.

Our next classes focused on the center's Spanish-speaking clients. Rebecca's limited Spanish didn't stop her. Working with the students in English and Spanish, the new little sewing community created a bilingual guide of sewing terms, a help to teacher and students alike. We developed a student agreement, asking prospective students to commit to the six weeks, to arrive on time, and to understand that they had a responsibility to the community if they expected to receive a sewing machine at the end.

When the program coordinator from the nearby Bayview Foundation called asking about classes, I talked with Rebecca. This would be yet another cultural shift. Although the Bayview community houses a diverse population, the folks interested in learning to sew were mainly Hmong, elders who had arrived in the United States in the tumult of the 1970s and the aftermath of the Vietnam War. I believed that the balm of sewing could offer one avenue of healing. Steeped in Hmong hand sewing traditions, working on a sewing machine was something new for this group of women. They approached the task undaunted, eager to learn.

Beginning classes in the Northport community a few years later brought another cultural shift. Newly arrived Afghan women dove into the sewing program. Considering the differences in dress between our cultures, Rebecca created a pattern for loose-fitting pants and tunics that were familiar to these students.

Rebecca built on Steff's strong foundation, tailoring each class to meet the needs and dreams of the students. A few common lessons were woven throughout—machine knowledge and simple upkeep, basic sewing principles, confidence on the machine, and paying it forward.

Paying it forward was an integral piece of local classes and any machine given away and carried through all of our work. In our local programs, we asked the center where the class was housed what they needed. The Catholic Multicultural Center needed fleece hats to give out to homeless clients in the winter. At Northport, they needed baby blankets for new mothers. At Bayview, they needed tote bags for senior members of the community.

Local programs continue to evolve as we add more centers, instructors, students, and glimpses of a broader world beyond our city. Our volunteers are integral as they show up each week to float in the classroom, helping anyone who raises a hand.

Bob Heideman, who breathed the inspiration for our local initiative, passed away in 2009. I have no doubt he is smiling.

An appearance on the Nancy's Corner of Sewing With Nancy highlighted the SeaHope Artists' Series.

When SeaHope relocated to Madison, all hands were on deck to cut out bags!

# Chapter 15

Wood and water filled my nose as I stepped into the Chauvin Brothers hardware store, my eyes adjusting to the dim light. Two men turned their weathered faces from their conversation with the man behind the counter regarding me, their expressions blank. As I drove into Chauvin, Louisiana, I noted boats abandoned along the bayou, names like *Sunset* and *Our Dream*, letters peeling from the hulls. I was in Cajun country.

Two months earlier, in April 2010, the Deepwater Horizon oil spill flooded the Gulf, forever changing the environment, communities, and lives. I was surprised when I received emails asking what The Sewing Machine Project planned to do about the disaster. Puzzled, I imagined a group of fishermen or oil rig workers standing around a pallet of sewing machines scratching their heads. My connection to Louisiana was more widely known than I had realized due to my many truckloads of sewing machines delivered after Hurricane Katrina. Sewing machines didn't feel like the answer this time. I wondered whether I was really the person to help.

I talked with Maggie, an extension agent in Terrebonne Parish, where BP was headquartered, in an effort to get a broader feel for the community beyond the headlines.

"People are suffering, Margaret," she said. "They have lost their jobs. Fishing is a way of life here. So is working on the oil rigs. Our way of life is sewn into the fibers of people here. You destroy the water, and people are lost." Maggie went on to describe community support groups growing like tender plants in the midst of the crisis—resources offering counseling and community meals.

"People are trying to help, but it's not easy. Everyone keeps to themselves here. Some know-it-all Yankee comes in and tries to tell them how to fix things, and they just don't trust. I know. This is my home, and this is how I was raised." Maggie's words let me glimpse a world that was foreign to me.

I let the questions swirl and began to imagine a product that could be sold to raise money, to offer jobs. What would be relevant? What would hold meaning?

I envisioned a messenger bag. We could gather old sails to use as fabric, asking sailors from Wisconsin to donate, a way to help in the face of a devastating crisis. We could add boat hardware and fishing net to echo the language of the sea.

*We could produce them in Terrebonne Parish*, my inner voice murmured excitedly. *We could create jobs and make money to give back to the community!* My pulse quickened as I began planning. I contacted area sailing clubs. Rolled and folded sails, no longer needed on mains and mizzens, appeared on my back porch. The fabric's crunch became familiar as I waded through the pile.

I planned a visit to Louisiana, with extra time scheduled to drive into Terrebonne Parish to meet people and shop for hardware. I called John Douthat, the owner of AllBrands Sewing in Baton Rouge. Years before, John and I had found one another after he read about The Sewing Machine Project and asked how he and his business could help. He had been a supporter and cheerleader ever since.

"You want to make the bags in Terrebonne Parish?" he'd said. "You should have industrial machines for working with that sail fabric. It's so tough and slippery. I'll connect you with Steve from Sailrite in Indiana."

Steve stepped into the conversation. "We can give you twelve machines," he said. "These are portable industrials. People use them for sail repair on their boats."

Within weeks, I was navigating Terrebonne Parish in a rental car. Chauvin was a foreign country, and I struggled to understand the thick Cajun tongue. I ignored the feeling I got as I met people— surface "Hello, honey," floated on an undercurrent of distrust.

Maggie explained, "This is an insulated culture. People are kind, and they will help you, but they will never really trust you. You're an outsider."

Walking into the hardware store, I felt the wall between myself and the grizzled men at the counter.

"Hi," I said as I approached them. "I am looking for boat hardware and fishing net." The man behind the counter cocked his head and said something, his molasses thick Cajun accent another language.

"Small things, like little pulleys or hooks," I continued, holding up my fingers measuring an inch.

He stepped out from behind the counter, his hand motioning me to follow. I could feel his friends' eyes on my back. We walked into the shadows of the old store. This place was clearly dedicated to the heavy fishing industry in the region, with an inventory geared toward boats. The creak of the worn, wide plank wood floor reminded me of my dad's hardware store, where I grew up working. I smiled at the memory, a mental note to tell him about this store, so different from the one he'd owned.

I was guided down an aisle near the back, bins of hardware lining the shelves. I dug into the bins and chose a few pieces, dropping them into the little brown bags piled nearby. The owner pointed to net on rolls suspended from the ceiling in every gauge imaginable for every size of fish. I pointed to one, and he unrolled a few yards. He cut a length for me and then another. I tucked my new treasures under my arm and followed him to the front counter.

I finished paying and thanked the owner, heading for the door. When I turned back to say goodbye, the men were already back in conversation. In their minds, I was already gone.

I drove down the finger of land, bayou on my left, until sea surrounded me on three sides. Men sat on fishing boats in dry docks, as if placed by habit on their decks, talking with one another.

French settlers named the area Terrebonne, "Good Earth," land rich in nature's resources. As I scanned the scene, I wondered about man's ability to use what the earth has to offer and make such a mess of her bounty.

I returned to Wisconsin with bits of netting and hardware, determined to continue planning. The messenger bag image became more and more clear in my mind's eye, the details filling in little by little. My friend Ann drew up a pattern. More sails arrived.

As I sat with my board of directors, my voice was clearly the most animated in the chorus. I was so sure it was a good idea. We chose SeaHope Partners as a name, an homage to the land and the sea, a nod to the hope we attempted to offer. Lois, a board member and graphic designer, designed a simple logo with a wave design. A local screen printer used this graphic to create patches to sew on each bag.

Steffani Lincecum and I traveled to Houma, Louisiana, in July to set up a test sewing room at Maggie's extension office, buoyed by an idea and optimism. The picture of how this would unfold was so clear in my mind. Maggie had gathered some retired sewers willing to help us pilot the project. The Sailrite machines arrived and sat boxed along the wall of the conference room we were to use. The pallet of home sewing machines and sails I'd shipped a few weeks earlier was parked outside the back door.

Steff and I met John Douthat and one of his technicians at the extension office on Sunday night when we arrived. John had kindly agreed to help us set up the industrial machines. Together the four of us set up ten machines on folding tables. As we worked, John explained the details of the powerful machines. One touch to the foot control, and they roared to life, moving at speeds I'd never encountered before. In the back of my mind, I wondered quietly whether their power would be daunting to our incoming team of sewers. I hushed my questions and focused on the work at hand.

On Monday morning, Maggie and her eight friends arrived with casseroles, salads, and pop, a celebratory vibe hanging in the air. Steff picked up and opened a two-liter bottle of Coke. "I call this 'sewing juice'!" she said, grinning. Our hearts and expectations were high.

Steff was no stranger to sewing rooms. As a costumer for movies and television in an earlier chapter of her life, she knew her way around the sewing industry and could teach and instruct our team in the work ahead. I stood on the sidelines as everyone listened to her instructions. "Margaret will be cutting out the pieces," Steff explained, "and I've written the pattern instructions on this whiteboard." She pointed to the large board with her neat writing and diagrams. "Take your time to get to know these machines," Steff continued. "They're powerful but not impossible! Learn to tame them so you can go at a comfortable pace. Be careful adding the trim. The black against white will really stand out, so the lines need to be straight! And Margaret and I are here if you have questions."

I set up shop on the floor and cut out the pattern pieces, the stiff sails slipping and sliding on the tile. The ladies got to work. Beginning on pieces of cotton, they tried out the powerful industrial machines, jumping when the machine took off at the mere tap of a foot. After acquainting themselves with the machines, we gave them each a pile of pattern pieces, the makings of a bag. The pattern was basic, but the fabric was a challenge. Sails slip and slide with a stiffness that makes them resistant to taming. I had tested the pattern at home using an old heavy-duty Singer and had not had much trouble. But the combination of the powerful sewing machines and the slippery, stiff fabric caused more than a few sideways glances. The ladies muttered to one another as they wrangled the pieces. My eyes met Steff's midway through the day, a note of worry passing between us.

On day two, fewer sewers showed up. Although the pallet of home sewing machines had been intended for delivery to families in the area, we unloaded them and set them up, taking down the industrial machines. Steff's voice was encouraging, while mine was a combination of frustration and worry as I noted the crooked lines and uneven stitches. The vision that had been sitting so solidly in my mind's eye was becoming hazy. I'd imagined finishing twenty or twenty-five bags during the week and hoped to sell them for over $100 each to make enough money to impact area groups. I was so sure it would work—the vision was so strong.

By day four, we only had two sewers. At the end of day five, our last day, we had three finished bags, their crookedly sewn lines making them unsaleable. Steff and I sat down with a glass of "sewing juice."

Exhausted and disappointed, I asked Steff, "What now?" I was so sure it would work.

"This is not an easy process," Steff agreed.

We considered options. Maybe a different group of sewers? Maybe a different pattern? And the bigger question—was this more than we could manage? It took strength to uproot an idea that had so firmly taken root. I wondered if we should completely pull it out and throw it away or prune it, maybe replant it. I needed time to think. I needed to go back home and report to the board. Embarrassed and defeated, I began to cry. Steff held me.

We hauled the industrial machines into a closet and cleaned up the home sewing machines, preparing them for delivery. The next day, Saturday, we took the machines to a town nearby where a local church hoped to start a sewing circle. Talking with the sewing teacher as we unloaded the machines, my mood was temporarily buoyed as I was reminded of the things we did well.

When I met with my board upon our return to Wisconsin, I pushed myself to share each detail, owning my frustration and miscalculation. It was difficult to meet the eyes of the board members.

"I thought it would work. I was so sure," I said quietly.

"Asking ourselves what is within and outside of our scope is part of our job," Jacqui, the board president, said. "Maybe setting up manufacturing is outside of our scope." Kindly, wisely, the board members each offered words of advice and consolation.

"I guess I could see if someone in Wisconsin could sew these bags," I said. "I just wanted to do it all. To create jobs and bring in money. I guess if someone here made them, we could still raise money for the groups affected by the spill. Just not make the bags there."

Board members nodded as we drew the lines of what we are and what we aren't. Yes, we offer sewing machines—creative tools that can open new doors. But setting up a sewing house and managing manufacturing is quite another thing. As we talked, the boundaries became easier to see.

After the meeting, I poured myself a cup of coffee—relieved, frustrated, and exhausted. And it occurred to me that we never asked the people of Houma whether they wanted us there. We never asked what THEY thought of the idea. We never asked whether a sewing house was an industry they'd be interested in or would appreciate. We worked with retired volunteer sewers, not even searching for the people who needed jobs. *I had decided I knew best about a culture of which I knew little.* Remembering the faces of the women sewing, I realized I'd never even asked them what they thought.

That night I dreamed that I was floating on my back on a narrow river. The water was just the right temperature, my body relaxed. As I floated downstream, I curved and turned with the water's narrow path. Gliding by an embedded rock, I grabbed for it and hung on tight, fighting to hang on in the moving water. I became tense and anxious and fought the river's pull to move me forward. Finally, I let go of the rock and continued to move with the flow of the water and was immediately calm.

I woke the next morning with a sense of cautious hope. We had sails and a good idea. What next? I began researching sewing houses in Madison, groups that made it their business to sew professionally for others. My vision began to shift. We could still sew the bags and sell them as a fundraiser for community groups in Louisiana.

I contacted Brown Sales, a local sewing house, and they agreed to sew the bags. A group of volunteers gathered to cut out the pattern pieces, and we worked together, cutting and marking the bags for delivery and construction.

A month later, I picked up the first load of finished bags, an audible sigh of relief surprising me. The bags were beautiful—expertly sewn and ready to sell. We created an independent website to market the bags, telling the story in well-chosen images. Shortly after the site went live, an artist from New Orleans called.

"You know, I would be happy to decorate a bag. One of a kind." Once again, my mind began to spin, and I reminded myself to be careful, but I agreed and spread the word among the arts community, asking others to embellish a bag. The response was joyfully positive. Everyone wanted a doorway to help. After sending flat pattern pieces to interested artists, the pieces returned stitched, painted, and printed, embellished in the artists' chosen medium. I delivered them carefully to Brown Sales, and the bags emerged, a one-of-a-kind "Artists Series."

Sales were strong, especially with the artists' bags. A local gallery asked to feature the bags in their storefront, and we sold more. Other galleries in different states did the same. The idea shifted in my head, reminding me that an idea has a life of its own.

When we recouped our expenses and gathered the $3,000 profit, I began researching community groups in Terrebonne Parish that fit our profile and were established after the spill to help the people of the region. A group called LossTalk piqued my interest. I read about their efforts to reach out to kids and adults, helping them gather and share their stories and helping them heal. They were small like us, and this felt like the right place. I called the group's founder, Kathy, to learn more and discuss a donation.

"I formed LossTalk to create channels for conversation during crises," she explained. "We serve kids and adults, facilitating conversation toward community and healing." I excitedly went to my board. "I think this is where we should donate the money," I said. "They are a small organization doing important work."

The board voted in agreement, and I flew to Louisiana to present a check and sewing machines to LossTalk. Kathy and I sat on her sweeping front porch drinking sweet tea as she shared personal stories of the group's struggles and triumphs.

"You have no idea how much this will help our group and our work," Kathy said.

The idea sat solidly in my mind's eye, an altered version of its original form, but now it felt it was as it should be.

Three months later, a letter arrived from a law firm in Houma explaining that LossTalk was a fraud. The founder, Kathy, had forged her credentials. The stories were her dreams but not reality. She had defrauded countless donors. I read and reread the letter in disbelief, dreading yet another difficult conversation with my board.

The following week, I sat before the board members, head hanging, admitting that I had misread Kathy's organization. I had messed up, again. Ashamed and defeated, the small but familiar voice of self-doubt taunted me. As I shared the story, board members gasped, sealing my disappointment.

When I arrived home later that day, I sat alone in the stillness, beating myself up. *Why did I think I could do this? Why did I start the SeaHope thing? Let's go back even further. Who did I think I was starting this organization?* No words of encouragement could pull me out of the hole I'd dug for myself.

Harking back to a practice I'd created out of necessity, I allowed myself to sit in the darkness for however long it took, reminding myself quietly that it would not be forever. When I would feel even an ounce of strength, I did one small thing. I took one small step up the ladder toward the light. And so it was. There was day-to-day work that needed to be done for The Sewing Machine Project. When a donation check arrived, the funds proved to me that someone still believed in what we were doing, even when I couldn't. When a note arrived sharing details of a group's efforts to help their community and their need for a sewing machine, I was reminded of the difference this tool could make. When a call came from a community group asking me to share the story of the organization, I remembered that there was a story to tell. The Sewing Machine Project's life continued, and it pulled me along.

When I opened a letter from the Houma attorneys and found a reimbursement check for the entire amount of our LossTalk donation, I gasped and began to cry. Somewhere inside me, a voice echoed, *You'll be okay.* I cautiously began again to search for a recipient and found Bayou Grace, checking and rechecking their credentials. With both an environmental and community focus, Bayou Grace rebuilt on many fronts. Rebecca, the director, and her father invited me down to talk and learn more about their work. We walked their land together. Standing atop the levee, they described the dramatic land loss due to climate change and man's manipulation of the waterways, their concern palpable as they surveyed the evolving landscape. They described the simple meal program they had set up in their local community center. Once a week, they offered a free meal, and each week a different agency helped out and shared its resources with the community. Food, counseling, and job assistance were all covered in those weekly meals. Although my trust felt shaky, I trusted that we had found the right place, and my board agreed.

I returned home and mailed them a check for $3,000.

Though we never really silence those voices that berate us for missteps, the critical voices inside me became, for the moment, quieter. We like to believe we're in control. We like to think we know the ending but never really do. I am reminded, again and again, that I am merely steering this idea, holding the tiller lightly. I know that I am on the right path.

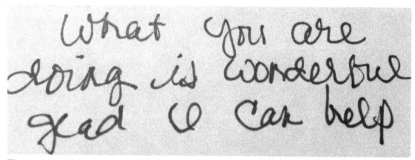

The words of supporters are a balm when I am looking for direction.

# Chapter 16

"Hi, welcome. Are you Margaret?" a woman in a well-tailored jacket extended her hand. I jockeyed to read her name tag.

"Hi, um, Pam, yes. Thank you. I'm glad to be here."

I was in Los Angeles at the invitation of the American Sewing Guild. The call had come several months earlier, asking if I would be willing to be the keynote speaker for their 2010 annual conference. I had accepted, happily surprised they were interested in hearing about The Sewing Machine Project. The annual gathering is a feast of color and inspiration as sewers from all over the country come together to connect, learn, and share a love of sewing.

I arrived a day early, giving me time to acclimate and make final preparations for my speech at the opening luncheon the next day. The city of Los Angeles and its towering Hyatt hotel were new territory. After settling into my hotel room, I wandered the maze of hallways, struggling to find the main ballroom where I would be speaking. I met Pam at the door.

Leading me into the ballroom, Pam turned and explained, "This is where you'll be tomorrow. Let me introduce you to Tim, our AV guy." She extended her arm, draped in a luscious fuchsia crepe, toward a young man making his way across the room.

Tim smiled as he shook my hand. "Do you have your PowerPoint saved on a thumb drive?" he asked. I dug in my purse to find it. The tiny stick felt weighty as I handed it to him. I always set up my own presentations, checking and rechecking the technology before every event. I'd felt so confident, but something in the transfer of my presentation into Tim's hands brought on uncertainty.

"I've never given away control of my presentation," I said, a worried note in my voice. "I usually use my own computer and projector, my own remote." Tim nodded, reassuring me that all would be well. His arm swept across the dining room's expanse. Over forty round tables dotted the landscape like boats moored in the harbor. The stage looked so far away—it could easily have been another country.

"We have a great system. Don't worry," Tim assured me. "I'll be in the back, in the booth." I followed his gaze to the back of the room. "And you'll have a remote."

"Okay," I murmured, wishing a bit of his confidence would seep beneath my skin.

I kept myself busy all afternoon. I'd signed up for a class in heirloom sewing and another in hand-stitched buttonholes. I relaxed into the familiarity of stitching, enjoying the community of sewers around me, and the heartfelt conversation that sewing evokes. My hands moved in creation, giving my mind a chance to rest.

I was registered for a variety of classes during the conference, the highlight being a session with Sandra Betzina directly following the luncheon at which I'd make my presentation. Sandra's relaxed approach to garment fitting and fabric had long been a trusted resource to me, her books tucked into the bookshelves of my sewing room. I couldn't wait to meet and work with her.

The next day, an hour before the luncheon, I arrived at the dining room. Banquet servers laid place settings and napkins and filled water glasses, the air tinkling with silverware's metallic music. I scanned the distance from front to back. The room was huge. All of the tables were set for the three hundred people expected to attend.

Lifting a glass of water from one of the tables, I took a sip and tried to still the nervousness in my stomach. *I am me*, the voice in my head said silently. I needed to remind myself.

"Margaret, you're here." I turned to see Pam entering the room. Her familiar face felt good. "Let me show you where we'll be sitting." She led me to a table in front of the stage. I laid my speech on a chair and draped a napkin over the back.

In ones and twos and threes, sewers flooded into the room, excitedly sharing what they'd learned that morning, eyes searching for others in their group. The room was filled with chatter.     I sat with the ASG board members, smiling and listening as they chatted over logistics and afternoon plans. I hoped they didn't notice my hands shaking. Reminding myself that I was speaking about something so familiar and important to me, I did my best to calm my nerves. After lunch, Pam introduced me while I stood at the side of the stage.

*Breathe*, my inner voice commanded. I stepped to the podium, leaning into the mic.

"My name is Margaret Jankowski, and I began The Sewing Machine Project in 2005," I began.

The first slide hovered behind me, larger than life. I clicked the remote, and an image of the headline that inspired me filled the screen. I went on, my voice gathering strength with each sentence as I looked from one face to the next, making eye contact. I clicked for the third slide, my voice growing stronger, then looked over my shoulder to check the screen. The slide had advanced on its own, and another took its place as I watched. What was happening?

"Hmm, the slides don't seem to be cooperating," I said, hoping Tim would take my cue and recognize the problem. But the island of the AV booth was miles away. The slides moved forward quickly behind me, no longer aligned with the words on my script. The remote, once a tool for navigation, was now useless in my hand. I kept talking, but my shaky foundation was slipping. My heart pounded as I struggled to breathe, and the words on the page blurred. I looked out over the faces, wondering if they understood.

*Pull yourself together*, my inner voice commanded, but my body was in panic mode. Inexperience and self-doubt, a wicked combination, consumed me. I prayed I'd make it through and kept going.

Holding back tears, barely meeting the eyes of the audience as I finished, I said, "Thank you," then turned and left the stage, returning to my seat. I'm sure people applauded, but I couldn't hear.

"That was wonderful," Pam patted my back. The rest of my table mates nodded. Trying to smile, I was sure they were lying. I pulled a tissue from my purse and dabbed my eyes.

The moment the luncheon ended, I said my goodbyes and burst through the lobby doors into the L.A. sunshine, taking deep gulps of air. The ground was moving beneath my feet like I'd just washed up on shore.

*Maybe I can just walk back to Wisconsin*, I thought. I sat on a bench on a busy L.A. street, wringing the tears out of me, feeling more alone than I could remember. Was this some kind of cosmic joke?

The universe testing me? I called my tried and true friend, Walt, and his voice comforted me.

"Oh, it can't be that bad," he said. "They probably didn't even notice."

"You weren't there!" I sniffed. "It was awful!"

"Well, what are you going to do?" he asked.

"I'm thinking of walking all the way home."

"Oh, brother. You are Margaret Jankowski. Get back in there!" he chided.

*There is no way I can go back inside,* I thought. Staying outside would mean missing Sandra Betzina's class. I would be embarrassed to be in there with all those people who had witnessed my disaster of a speech. I walked for three hours in downtown L.A. in a cloud of shame and sadness that I couldn't shake. As the sun dipped behind the tall buildings and a coolness settled in, I headed back to the hotel.

I walked into the front lobby, navigating the field of temporary signs marking the pathways to conference workshops. One sign read "Sandra Betzina," with an arrow pointing down the hall. Though I knew the class had ended a half hour before, I decided to wander down that way and peek into the room. The classroom door stood ajar. Chairs askew, the room held echoes of the inspiration I'd missed. Sandra moved about, packing up samples and books. I watched without a word. After a few minutes, she turned and regarded me, her face calm and open.

"Hi, I was supposed to be in your class," I said.

"Oh, are you Margaret?" she inquired. "Your name was the only one not checked off on my list."

"Yes," I said, and then it spilled out. "I spoke at the luncheon today and messed up. I needed the afternoon to take a walk."

"Oh, I'm sorry I missed your talk," she replied. "I was down here setting up."

"I drowned," I mumbled, studying my feet.

"Really? It couldn't have been that bad," she said warmly.

"I'm pretty sure it was."

"Tell you what, I just have a few more things to pack. How about you help me, and we'll go get a glass of wine?"

I stepped to the front of the room, carefully packing a box with books, her familiar face on the back cover. After we finished, we walked to the lobby bar, took a seat, and ordered a glass of cool, fragrant Sauvignon Blanc. As I sipped my wine, I relaxed and told Sandra Betzina about The Sewing Machine Project. It was the truest telling of the story I'd ever delivered.

She nodded with understanding, "I get it. A sewing machine can change a life."

"I just feel so bad about today," I said. "I am used to speaking to groups of twenty people or so, and this, well, it was so many people. I was so nervous! And nothing worked right. They chose me to do this, and I let everyone down."

"I'll bet people will remember your story," she replied. "Trust me. They weren't as affected by the messed-up slides as you were. They don't know what your presentation was supposed to look like."

And in that moment, I once again knew without a doubt that I was exactly where I was supposed to be. There had been a deeper lesson about trusting and finding my feet. I'd read a quote by Anne Lamott once that said, "Grace bats last," and again and again, I know that this is true. I'd sailed into the unknown, capsized, and found the surface with the help of Walter's prodding and Sandra Betzina's kind invitation. There would be more missteps and troubling moments, to be sure, but in that moment, I was saved again.

St. Joseph's Day is a spectacle of color and sound when the Indians appear at night.

# Chapter 17

The man behind the truck stop counter eyed me carefully, ringing up my purchases one by one—soda, pretzels, a road atlas. It was Sunday morning, and I could see his friends had joined him for coffee and local gossip. They stood around the counter in seed caps and twill jackets, plaid shirts peeking out from underneath.

"So where ya from?" His voice was spread thick with Missouri.

"Madison, Wisconsin," I replied.

"You've come this far without a map?" he asked.

"Yep."

"So what'd ya do, just get in and start driving?" His friends chuckled, tipping their cap brims as I picked up my purchases.

"Yep, pretty much."

The bell on the door dinged as I stepped outside. Martha waited in the truck.

"Margie, I'd like to see where we're going," she'd murmured as we pulled into the truck stop.

I was accustomed to traveling this route, threading south from Madison to Barrington, Illinois, west to St. Louis, south to Memphis, and on to New Orleans. I handed Martha the atlas. She opened to Missouri, dragging her finger to Cooter, our current location.

A physical map shows us where to go and where we've been. As we travel, we create another internal map, marking places we discover that hold meaning, creating a constellation that guides us. My trips to New Orleans, each a journey into the unknown, marked new locations on the physical map while my internal map lit up with new adventures, new stories, and new truths about the landscape of myself.

I had the map of New Orleans ready in my backpack. My map had been folded and refolded many times, becoming more pliable with each visit to show where each day would take me. Often traveling solo and without GPS, I would position the map on the seat beside me, using it to guide me through neighborhoods with tangled streets I would gradually learn to navigate. Each point on my map was a story.

On an earlier visit, I'd driven my van filled with machines to East New Orleans in search of Einstein Charter School. Serving a largely Vietnamese population, the teachers at Einstein hoped to provide post-trauma therapy in the wake of Hurricane Katrina. The staff had planned a quilt, each square a child's memory, penned in colored marker on muslin. They'd asked for machines to stitch the memories together.

Driving to Einstein School, I struggled to read my map in quick glances as I drove, my eyes drawn in every direction by the watery devastation. I got lost after missing an exit and pulled over to take a closer look at the map, temporarily parking next to a tangle of vines and debris. A sign reading "Closed for the Season" rose out of the green as if escaping the vines' grasp. Raising my eyes, I saw the bones of an amusement park, rusted and skeletal, a behemoth tangled in the chaos. Like archaeological sites, these landmarks of an earlier time lived on no map, populating the landscape as haunting reminders.

Many schools and community centers requested sewing machines as New Orleans came back to life. These deliveries took me away from the more familiar city center. My map was a trusted and necessary tool. Einstein in the East, O'Perry Walker across the river, New Orleans Recreation Department in Gentilly, my map's folds belied its use.

Even destinations within the city could be a challenge as I wove the truck through pitted, narrow streets. Signs were often twisted or not there at all. On one visit, I arrived at McDonogh 42 Elementary Charter School and waited by the large iron gate for instructions. Cherice and her mother, Mrs. Harrison, suggested I contact the school.

"They need books," Mrs. Harrison said, and Cherice nodded.

"School libraries really suffered in the storm."

I had mentioned this to my friend Dell, a teacher in the Madison schools. Dell was interested in what was going on in New Orleans. At the same time, Dell and his colleagues were concerned about the hundreds of books still in good condition that the Madison schools were discarding. They had formed the Book Rescuers, packing up the orphan books to donate without knowing where they would go. I met the group before leaving for New Orleans, and we loaded forty boxes of books into the back of the rental truck, nestling them in among the sewing machines.

The school librarian walked across the playground and opened the gate.

"Hi, welcome. You can drive right in here. I'll get some kids to help you unload."

I eased the truck up the curb and into the schoolyard. Seven boys and girls in light blue and gray uniforms poured out of the door into the sunlight, gathering near the back of the truck on the playground. I unclipped the back latch and hoisted the heavy metal door. The ramp complained as I wrenched it out, extending and dropping it on the ground with an ornery thud. Up and down the ramp, the kids unloaded the truck one box at a time, taking the books to the library with the librarian orchestrating the placement of each box. Following the kids up the stairs, I got a good look at the school and its library, noting the care that came from salvaging things you love. Pictures were tacked to the walls. An awards case stood empty. The library's shelves gradually filled with books.

"These books came from Madison schools," I said as the librarian surveyed the room. "Teachers packed them up to send to you."

"We are most grateful," she replied.

Waving goodbye to our team of helpers, I carefully pulled out of the yard, the iron gate swinging closed with a loud clank, locking behind me. I marked the school on my map. An invisible thread now connects the two schools, one in Madison and one in New Orleans.

My New Orleans map lay on the kitchen counter that evening as I studied the next day's route. I was staying at Cathy Nelson's home near the racetrack in New Orleans' Gentilly neighborhood. Cathy had walked into Hans' one day, answering a question I'd yet to voice aloud. After learning that the hotels in New Orleans could no longer offer me a free room, I wondered where I could stay when visiting the city to deliver machines. Our tiny budget could not bear hotel costs. Cathy, a slight, pale woman with eyes that sparkled, came through the front door of the store, businesslike as she approached the counter.

"Are you Margaret?" she asked.

"Yes."

"I've heard about the work you do. You go to New Orleans, right?"

I nodded.

"I have a house down there. If you ever need a place to stay, you can use my house."

I took Cathy up on her offer, staying in her cozy Gentilly home on many visits to New Orleans. Sometimes I was there with Cathy and her family, but often, Cathy left a key with a neighbor, and I had the house to myself.

Cathy and her cousin Maggie sat at the kitchen counter with me that evening. We pored over the map as I charted the next day's course.

"I need to deliver a few machines within the city," I said, "and one over in Slidell. I'm not sure I can do all of that in one day."

"We'll go to Slidell for you!" the ladies chimed.

Our fingers grazed the map from New Orleans to Slidell. I gave them Beverly's address. Beverly was an older lady who had not been able to make it to the church on distribution day. When we talked on the phone, she shared her sewing history.

"I've sewn all my life," she said. "My mother and grandma taught all of us to sew. My machine was ruined in the storm."

I knew an experienced seamstress would appreciate the Bernina 830 I had in the truck. Solid and powerful, with a reliable stitch, the 830 in its red case is cherished in the sewing world. We loaded the machine into Cathy's trunk.

The next evening, we compared notes, sharing stories of the day's deliveries. I marked each stop on my map. A quiet smile swept across Cathy's face.

"Oh, Margaret, I'm so glad we had the chance to meet Beverly," she said. Maggie nodded in agreement.

Together they shared Beverly's story. Growing up in New Orleans as one of twelve kids, Beverly and her brothers and sisters learned to sew out of necessity, clothing the sizable family. Her mother and grandma, both accomplished seamstresses, set up an assembly line with two treadle machines. The twelve children each had their roles as their family "factory" churned out clothing, bedding, and curtains for the household. Beverly shared a story about seeing a dress she loved in a downtown department store. She'd known better than to ask to try it on—people of color were not allowed to do so. She looked it over carefully, noting its lines and seams, then hurried outside. Beverly sat on the sidewalk, her back against the building, knees tucked up as a writing desk, and sketched the dress with enough detail that her grandma could make it for her.

Beverly was delighted when she clicked open the red case. "I can't wait to start sewing again."

Each trip to New Orleans created more markers, more points on the map. I revisited past recipients, now friends, to say hello and check on them and their machines. I introduced myself to new friends, each person a star on the physical map and the map within me.

Prior to her death on Mardi Gras Day in 2009, I had never missed a chance to visit with Miss Antoinette at the Mother-in-Law Lounge. She was one of the brightest stars. Perched on a barstool enjoying the red beans and rice that always seemed to be simmering or serving beer behind the bar when Antoinette needed a rest, I always felt welcome in her presence.

Years later, my friend Ann and I would set out to find the Indians on St. Joseph's Day, and Miss Antoinette's bar was as good a place as any to start. Pulling up near the bar, Ann and I got out of the truck and stood beneath the highway, listening. St. Joseph's night is tradition for the Mardi Gras Indians, their full suits and rituals on display more for one another than the outside world. Moving through the streets in formation, the chief determines the route. The spy boy runs ahead to search for other gangs. A parade of followers typically joins in, carried by the rhythm of the drums, hoping to witness the rituals between the gangs.

The trick is to find the Indians.

Ann and I stood in front of the bar and listened without knowing what exactly we were listening for. A rustle of feathers, and an Indian turned the corner. We followed at a respectable distance. Soon others appeared, greeting one another before moving together into the darkness of the dimly lit street. Feathers shifted, beads glinted under the street lamps, and the slow drumming quickened as the chanting grew louder. Our feet lifted in rhythm, propelled by the drums. Another group, all in yellow, approached, and we watched as they bowed and wove around one another, performing rituals older than we knew. Following into the darkness, we were part of a larger group now, bodies moving with the drumming, turning here and there, deeper and deeper into the neighborhood's streets.

"Do you know where we are?" Ann asked, and I shook my head and smiled. We were off any map we knew, buoyed by a trust that we would find our way home. Hours later, we stood under the highway in a blur of color, immersed in drums and chants reverberating from the concrete.

When we finally walked to the car at the end of the night, words escaped us. We both knew we would never forget that evening. Arriving home, I drew a new swath of stars, marking where we had walked. This was where we were. This was where we met the Indians.

Martha's finger traced the route on the freshly opened pages of our new atlas as we sat in the truck in Cooter, Missouri.

"Looks like we go this way," she said.

"Yes."

We drove south, following a meandering line that was at once familiar and new. My mind flooded with the many stories from previous trips to New Orleans, the stretches into the unknown, the moments of serendipity, and the surprises along the way. I can't help but wonder what this new journey will bring. As The Sewing Machine Project charts its own course, I gently guide it, letting it guide me.

MARGARET JOHN JANKOWSKI

The challenges offered at mending are a big part of the fun!

# Chapter 18

"I'm wondering if you can fix my pocket?" The man's face was a pale question mark, a map of life-to-date lined with crevices and scars. Slowly he pulled his arms out of the sleeves and laid his army jacket before us on the table.

"May I take a look?" I asked, feeling the need to request permission to touch his beloved garment. He nodded. My fingers grazed the olive canvas. Once a young, strong protector against the elements, the coat now lay aged and limp in my hands. Cigarettes and sweat emanated from each fiber, escaping like a cloud as I turned it over to inspect the pocket.

The dense stitching had torn away, taking a shred of the coat's foundation with it. A hole remained where the piece had been, like a window with a view to the inside.

I looked into his tired face.

"What is your name?" I asked.

"Jim."

"Jim, I'm Margaret. I'll need to patch the hole, and then I can sew the pocket back on. Does that sound okay to you?"

He nodded. "So you think you can fix it?"

I smiled. "Sure I can. There's a chair right there if you'd like to sit down." He pulled the orange plastic chair to the other side of the table and lowered himself into it, a sigh escaping as he settled into the seat, his elbow resting on the workspace.

Carefully clipping the threads, I nudged the torn fabric away from the pocket, examining it for signs of life. The ragged edges were feathery and worn, a thin shadow of the original fabric. I searched for a patching fabric that felt similar in color and weight. A piece of olive cotton did the trick. I positioned a small piece into the hole in the jacket, rotating it to find its best placement.

"I'm going to sew this little piece onto some denim," I said as he watched my hands move. "Then I'll sew the denim to the inside of the coat and let this little piece show through." He nodded, trusting.

"I think this way we'll have the strongest mend. And it'll look pretty good," I said.

He smiled. Setting my machine on a zigzag, I carefully stitched the jacket patch to the worn soft denim.

"You know, my mom sewed when I was a kid," he said. "She taught my sister to sew. Not me." He watched the needle move through the fabric.

The library, lit for reading, makes a perfect place to mend. The mending idea was Bird's, an SMP board member and fiber artist. Bird had read about the work of the artist Michael Swaine, who wheeled a treadle sewing machine around San Francisco's Tenderloin District, offering free mending. A performance art piece at first, he identified a deep well of need.

We set up our first mending site at a local community center, offering two hours of repairs on the first and third Wednesday nights of each month. A sign on the table announced, "Free Mending, 6–8 P.M." Aligning with the center's free meal program and food pantry hours, we positioned ourselves right in the middle of the action, and the program took off. Over the months, we gained the trust of the people we met and worked the bugs out of our program. After a year, we added a second site at Madison's Central Library. Situated downtown, and offering plenty of resources for people needing a fresh start, the Central Library site took off right away. A year later, we set up a third site at The Beacon day center, a community resource for people experiencing homelessness. The program grew yet remained simple. We established our ground rules:

Two volunteers at the table to mend, to talk with clients, to share ideas.

The schedule is first, third, and fifth weeks of the month rather than every other week, which can be confusing.

Only work that can be completed in the two-hour mending window is accepted.

Nothing is to be taken home by volunteers.

Volunteers are empowered to say no if a job is too time-consuming or complicated.

Anyone is welcome to have something mended.

If a client shows up with a whole stack of mending, volunteers can take just a few pieces, asking the client to return on a future date.

The rules, empowering and freeing, stuck, and the mending continued.

"I mean, I can sew a button on, but that's about it," Jim went on, his eyes looking off into the distance.

I took the patched piece from the machine bed, snipping the threads and inspecting it.

"I live with my sister now," he said. "She lets me stay in her spare room." His resting hand clenched tightly.

I pinned the patch to the inside of the jacket, carefully positioning the scrap to peer through the window of the tear. I eased the pins holding the patch in place.

"I don't sew, but I like to write," he went on. I nudged the fabric under the needle and lowered the foot. Reverse, then forward, I stitched a large perimeter, catching the edges of the patch. I smiled with satisfaction, noticing the thread's close match.

"Sometimes I take my typewriter out into the yard. I have a chair and a TV tray out there," Jim continued. "I just listen and write poetry." His words transported me to his makeshift office under the trees. The needle zigzagged the patch to the jacket's threads.

"I'm not right in the head—at least that's what my sister says." Jim's eyes met mine, and he looked down at the project. "That's looking pretty good."

"It is, right?" I pinned the corner of the patch in place on the newly fortified fabric. "We're down to the last step." I stitched the pocket in place, running the needle back and forth to hold the corner tight. Pulling the jacket out and snipping the threads, I placed it between us on the table for Jim to inspect. "What do you think?" I asked.

Jim's tired fingers swept the familiar fabric. "Oh, this is great," he said. "I think I'll get a few more years out of it." Jim stood and slowly put his arms through the sleeves. "Mind if I sit here awhile?"

"Not at all," I said.

Jim slid his chair to the side as a heavyset woman walked up to the table.

"I wonder if you can fix this?" She dropped several loaded shopping bags on the floor and held out a dog collar. The collar, a faded blue, rested oily in my hands.

She reached into her pocket and pulled out a metal D-ring. "This fell off," she said, placing it on the table.

"I can fix it," I said. "Have a seat. What is your name?"

"Jackie," she said, "and my dog's name is Spud."

"Jackie, I'm Margaret. Let's get Spud's collar put back together." I curled the webbing through the D-ring and pinned it in place. I threaded the machine with blue thread as Jackie eased herself into one of the plastic chairs. She shifted, searching for comfort.

"Spud's tied up outside," she said, "with a rope. I hope nobody takes him. He's my best friend."

"I can get this done pretty quick," I said, lowering the needle into the webbing. I stitched back and forth.

"You know, Spud knows when I'm having a bad day," Jackie said. "He stays real close like he's worried about me."

"What a good dog," I murmured. Lifting the presser foot, I slid the collar out and clipped the threads, releasing it from the machine's grasp. I pushed the collar toward her for inspection. "There you go," I said. "That should work."

"Thanks," said Jackie. She stood slowly and picked up her bags.

"Say hi to Spud for me," I said as she neared the door.

Jackie pulled her coat around her, the plastic bags shifting. "Thank you, I will," she said.

Jim looked at me from his sideline seat, opening his eyes as if waking from a dream.

"I had a dog once," he said. I smiled. He leaned back and closed his eyes as if resuming his dream. A tiny smile whispered across his lips as a young boy and his dog ran through his memory—carefree, moving easily, the early chapters of a life.

I looked over at Kate, my mending partner, as she hemmed a pair of khaki pants. Her client, a slight Asian man, watched her intently as she skillfully moved the pants through the machine. The old Singer slowed and stopped, then Kate pulled the pant leg off and snipped the threads. She held them up. "There, all done."

The man rose, bowing and taking the pants. Holding them up to gauge the new length, he nodded vigorously and smiled.

"Yes, yes," he said and bowed again.

Mary, our library liaison, popped her head in the door.

"How's it going?"

"Great!" Kate and I sang in unison, jostling Jim's eyes open.

"Would you consider doing this every week?" Mary asked.

"If we have enough volunteers," I replied.

"That would be great. We always have people asking when you'll be here. This service is such a godsend to so many. We offer lots of resources, and mending is a favorite."

Kate and I began our clean-up, folding scraps of denim, lining up thread and supplies, and guiding pins into the pin cushion. We cleaned and unplugged the machines and put them on the library cart, ready for storage.

Kate's client carefully folded his pants and waved goodbye. Jim slowly got up and smoothed his jacket.

"I might have some other things to mend," he said. "Is it okay if I come back?"

"Of course," I replied. "It might not be us the next time you come, but you are always welcome. We'd love to see you again."

Jim smiled, the crevices of his face following the curve of his lips.

"Okay, I'll see you again," he said. He walked through the door, turned to look back through the window, and raised his hand slowly in a goodbye.

Artists Big Chief Howard Miller and Queen Rukiya Brown are integral in the
New Orleans community, sharing and living cultural traditions.

Rukiya's "White Buffalo" suit was
purchased by Paris's Quai Branly
Museum.

Through education, artistry and
community service, Big Chief Howard
Miller passes along the traditions
and art of the Indian culture to future
generations.

# Chapter 19

*"Even though my artwork is in galleries and museum collections, my biggest pleasure is cultural ritual which happens during Carnival and on Mardi Gras Day. My suit, the Phoenix, tells about the history of our great city, and no matter the hardships "Still we rise." My White Buffalo suit is about peace. Stop the gun violence which has taken many lives here in my city. I'm that big queen that rides the white buffalo. People mask for all kinds of reasons, but when I put on my suit, I am honoring my ancestors and reaching out to touch people's spirits. When I mask, I am really taking the mask off. I am American Indian."*

-BIG QUEEN RUKIYA, CREOLE WILD WEST

Pulling up to the park shelter, I nodded to myself as I read the sign, "A.L. Davis Park." I was scheduled to meet Queen Rukiya and Chief Howard on yet another visit to New Orleans. I didn't know either of them. With no map beside me, I was testing my internal

GPS, a compass I was learning to trust, as I made my way through the city to the park.

My shoulders relaxed when I read the sign and saw Big Chief Howard and Big Queen Rukiya of the Creole Wild West gang seated at a picnic table. Cherice had connected us. After eight years of collaboration on sewing machine distribution, Cherice was pulled in too many directions. Her work with schools and literacy, as well as her art and cultural direction, consumed much of her time. She asked if I'd mind working with someone else in the Mardi Gras Indian community on sewing machine distribution. The change would free up her time and allow me to broaden my understanding of the scope of the Indian culture.

"You'll like working with Rukiya," Cherice said, and her mother, Herreast, nodded.

I got out of the car and walked toward the table. Howard stood, tall and elegant.

"Chief Howard? Queen Rukiya?"

They both nodded.

"An excellent connection," was how Cherice described these new partners. Rukiya Brown and Howard Miller, organizers in the Indian community, knew many masking Indians who could use a machine. Howard's most recent work with the New Orleans Mardi Gras Indian Council was focused on establishing a meeting space for all Indians. This was a revolutionary and necessary idea, given the distinct separateness between the individual gangs and the secrecy surrounding their suits' creation. I'd winced when Cherice first used the term "gangs" to describe separate Indian groups. She explained that the term emerged when longshoremen in New Orleans first developed these Indian groups out of long-standing friendships. "Gang" wasn't used negatively but rather as a term of camaraderie between men. The center that Howard had organized would be open to all groups of Indians, all gangs. It was a space for problem-solving, education, and teaching the important traditions asking to be remembered.

"I'm Margaret," I said, extending my hand. "The machines are in the car." Easily and slowly, Rukiya and Howard walked with me to the car to see the machines and help me unload. Their easy pace helped relax me, and I took a deep breath. By the time we had all ten machines lined up on the grass near the picnic table, my rhythm more closely mirrored theirs.

One by one, the Indians arrived. Rukiya contacted ten people for the ten machines I had promised to deliver.

"I'm Leroy," a tall gentleman introduced himself. Each introduction unfolded into a story as the Indians shared a bit of themselves— their gang, their rank. I was curious, and they kindly educated me on their role in the community, their pride radiating.

Between visitors, I sat beside Rukiya at the picnic table, enjoying the cool shade of an old oak tree. With long, heavy, braided hair, and a colorful scarf woven between her tresses, Rukiya exuded calm, her voice soothing, as she educated me about the Indians I was meeting. There was no need to stress or be anywhere but right here. Howard gently greeted my questions with respectful answers, as if every question was important. I was curious to know more about the center they were completing and the creative classes they would offer. I wanted to hear more about their own lives. Howard has been masking for decades and is a champion of the Mardi Gras Indian traditions, speaking on the national stage about the deep meaning of the culture. Rukiya is a renowned artist, showing her work in galleries internationally. When I zeroed in on these exhibitions,

Rukiya was quick to correct. "Margaret," she said, "national and international galleries are interested in my work. But I want my work with the people. When I mask and am in the community, I am bringing my art to the people."

"Will you need a set of sewing machines for the center classroom? We could bring them once the room is ready."

The morning slipped by, and one by one, the machines were picked up, loaded into cars, and onto buses to begin a new chapter. When we rose to say goodbye, Rukiya wrapped me in a hug, spicy and warm. Howard smiled, and I reached up to hug his tall frame.

We deeply thanked one another. I lowered myself into my rental car and took one last look at the two of them. They stood, smiling, under the trees, and waved a casual hand as I pulled away from the curb. On the seat beside me, I noticed my map peeking out of the pocket of my backpack. Leaving it folded, I made my way through the city.

MARGARET JOHN JANKOWSKI

The Houston delivery came together so quickly due to the cooperation of "sew" many!

# Chapter 20

"I'll wait here," Kim said as I pulled the truck into the no-parking zone and put on the flashers. Bending the rules had become a rule of its own.

"Don't let anyone take our truck!" I said, laughing.

My traveling companion on this trip in November 2017 was Kim Miller, a friend and SMP board member. We'd begun in New Orleans, delivering machines to Howard and Rukiya, and then traveled to Houston. Throughout the trip, we had been mistaken for twins—or at least sisters.

I zipped up my raincoat against the relentless rain, adjusting the hood around my face.

This time our U-Haul truck held one hundred sewing machines, boxed and ready for delivery. We were parked in a no-parking zone in front of Houston's George R. Brown Convention Center. We looked at each other and shrugged.

The George R. Brown in Houston's business district spans several city blocks, so huge it can house multiple conventions at one time. Colorful banners for the 2017 International Quilt Festival draped the front entrances. Festival flags hung limp in the pouring rain on poles up and down the street. The event is legendary, a gathering of quilters and sewing enthusiasts from all over the world. The festival is an annual feast of inspiration and a place for new ideas, techniques, and products.

We were honored to be invited to set up a booth in the nonprofit section. I spent months updating our displays and materials to prepare for this show. Sewers understand the value of a sewing machine, and we were eager to share our story. This group would most certainly understand our work.

When Hurricane Harvey dropped over sixty inches of rain on Houston only months before, I wondered if the show would be canceled. The Convention Center had opened its doors, becoming a city of the displaced. Only a few short weeks before our arrival, the facility was emptied and cleaned in preparation for the quilt show.

Watching the news from my home in Wisconsin as Harvey roared through, I recalled the devastation I had seen in New Orleans after Hurricane Katrina and was heartsick. Once again, that tiny voice whispered, "How can I help? Will they need sewing machines?"

I wrote to sewing machine manufacturers—a short, direct message suggesting they pack some extra machines to donate to our efforts when they packed their show materials, shipping them as part of their regular setup.

"I'll pick up the machines in Houston," I offered. "You can ship them right to the convention center."

Responses trickled in. Baby Lock agreed to send an extra pallet of twenty-five machines. Bernina agreed to send machines to AllBrands' location in Houston. John Douthat, the owner of AllBrands, agreed to donate some of his inventory.

"We'll have some Janome machines for you," John said. "They will be at the Houston store along with Bernina's machines. You can pick them all up there."

I'd made the hope-filled suggestion, only half believing anyone would respond. I had become familiar with the energy that bounces around an idea. Once I began thinking about gathering and distributing machines in Houston, the pieces, at least in my mind, began to fall into place. A plan began to take shape. One month before the show opened, I had a promise of 125 sewing machines. The question shifted from, *How do I get machines?* to *How do I find the people who need them?* Bringing sewing machines to the wet, weary city felt somewhat premature. More immediate needs were pressing, and many people were still displaced.

*But this is the timing we have,* I thought. *I'll see what I can find.* I studied a map of the greater Houston area. Overlaid with the most heavily impacted areas after the storm, the picture narrowed. Another overlay showed income levels, and the picture changed again. My finger landed on Northeast Houston. While 125 machines seemed like a large number to me, given the city's size, it was small. I focused on community centers, knowing they are hubs, especially in challenging times. I brought up a list of centers in the northeast corner of the city and scrolled through. Each center's profile described its services and had a photo of its coordinator. One after another, I read through the descriptions and studied the faces. One face seemed to call out to me. Tiffany. I dialed the number.

"Hello, this is Tiffany," she answered.

"Hi, my name is Margaret, and I am the director of a group called The Sewing Machine Project." I went on to tell her about our work.

"I will be in Houston next month. Do any of your clients need a sewing machine?"

Tiffany's voice changed, and her breath caught.

"Oh, my God. We have a sewing group right here at the center," she said. "It's a mess around here. Eighty-five percent of our clients are still in shelters." Her voice broke. "I'm sorry I'm crying," she sniffed. "My first day back to work, when I drove through the neighborhood, I couldn't believe it. I thought, *These people lost everything, and they didn't have much to start with.* Most of the ladies lost their sewing machines. And those machines were so important to them."

"I'd be happy to bring you some machines," I responded.

"Miss Margaret, you have no idea what a gift this will be. These ladies love to sew. They need to sew. And Harvey took their machines." Tiffany and I set a delivery date.

I called the American Sewing Guild's Houston chapter and talked with the president. She knew of a local 4-H chapter that needed machines.

"We can get those for you," I promised.

In an unfamiliar city, distances and travel times are a guess, points on a map, new and strange. Kim and I picked up the U-Haul at ten in the morning and began by driving out to AllBrands. The one hundred boxed machines were piled high around the perimeter of a tiny space in the back of the store. A group of quilters sat wedged in around a table, stitching and talking. Curious about what we were doing, we became the morning's entertainment, sharing details of the sewing machine distribution and the broader work of The Sewing Machine Project. I asked Kim to check one of the boxed machines, and she picked up sewing scissors from the table to open the box. An audible gasp escaped the stitchers.

"Oh, Kim, don't use that scissors," I said. "Here's a box cutter."

Turning to the ladies, I smiled. "She's not a sewer." Satisfied with my explanation, the ladies excused Kim for the high crime of almost using sewing scissors on cardboard.

We gradually loaded the truck, emptying the room of machines, and said goodbye to the sewers. We moved quickly as clouds formed on the horizon, warning of impending rain. I wondered what the sky had looked like months before as Harvey approached.

We drove to the George Brown, our second stop, to pick up the Baby Lock machines. That was where we were to meet Brenda, the 4-H leader who needed sewing machines. Arriving just as the rain escalated, I pulled up in the no-parking zone and found the button to start the flashers. Kim stayed in the truck while I ran inside, clutching the paperwork for the Baby Lock machines. The cavernous hall echoed with a pre-setup hollowness as I located the Baby Lock booth space. Our pallet, clearly labeled, sat off to one side. A woman in a Convention Center uniform drove up in a golf cart.

"Can I help you?" she asked.

"These machines were shipped here for my group, The Sewing Machine Project," I said, pointing to the label on the pallet.

"I can't just let you take them," she said, shaking her head. "You'll need a release."

I checked my watch. My schedule hadn't allowed time for standing around in the convention center. We were due in one hour at our community center stop, and it was pouring rain outside. I called my contact at Baby Lock, grateful he picked up, and handed the phone to the woman. She nodded as he explained the donation.

"Okay," she said, handing the phone back. She smiled, "Let's get you some help." Her smile pushed a sigh from my lungs.

I leaned in and gave her a hug. "Thank you so much."

A uniformed man appeared with a pallet jack, effortlessly lifted the pallet, and followed me across the huge hall. I pointed through the rain at our truck, grateful it was still across the street and not towed out of the no-parking zone. Ignoring the rain, he wheeled the pallet to the truck as Kim hopped out of the passenger seat, adjusting her hood. She unclipped the back latch, pushing the heavy door upward, and we all worked to transfer the machines from the pallet to the truck.

"Thank you so much!" I shook our helper's hand. He disappeared quickly back into the convention center.

I turned to see a car pull up behind the truck. A woman got out, pulling her raincoat tight around her. "Brenda?" I said.

She smiled and nodded.

"These machines are a godsend," she said as we loaded ten machines into her trunk.

"We lost our entire building, sewing machines and all. These will help our kids get back on their feet. They love to sew." Locking the trunk, Brenda got back into her car and pulled away.

"Okay, we'd better get going," I said, noting the time. It was four o'clock. We had agreed to be at the Northeast Community Center at four thirty.

"Let's get the truck closed up and get on our way."

We both looked up to see the tiny tail of the strap, lodged inside the back door housing, far out of our reach.

"I'm sorry I shoved the door up so hard," Kim said, shaking her head.

I smiled a tense smile. While I completely understood, I also worried about keeping our schedule. "I know. It's not your fault. I don't know what to do." We stood inside the back of the truck, looking out at the brightening sky as the rain let up, willing an answer.

A compact car pulled up behind us.

"Hi there," a woman said, getting out of the car. Noting the stress on our faces, she asked, "What's going on?"

We both pointed up at the door. "It's stuck," we said in unison.

"Well, sounds like you need a tall guy. My husband can help you. He'll be here in just a minute." Just then, a tall, lanky man arrived. "They need some help," she said, pointing at our two hopeful faces.

With a long-legged stride, the man stepped effortlessly into the back of the truck and stretched a long arm up to the door frame, easily reaching the strap. He wiggled it a bit and smiled. "Is that all you need?" he asked.

Kim and I laughed as the tension flooded out of our bodies and poured on the ground. "Thank you," we sang in a chorus.

I called Tiffany on our way. "Hi, Tiffany, this is Margaret. We had a bit of a delay. We'll be a little late."

Tiffany's voice lit the line. "Oh, don't worry. We're here. The ladies are so excited. They've been here for hours."

Following her directions, we exited the highway, winding through the neighborhoods to the center. The lawns of the tiny homes were washed canvases, littered with the storm's debris. Mud caked the road. Piles of wet, moldy furniture and mattresses lined the street, remnants of households destroyed. We drove in silence.

This is what you don't see in the news—familiar pieces of people's lives soaked and discarded, waiting to be carted away. I thought of

Tiffany's words: "These people lost everything, and they didn't have much to start with."

We pulled into the Northeast Community Center parking lot. A low, block building, the center welcomed us with a banner reading, "We're glad you're here."

Tiffany walked out to meet us. I knew her from the picture that had first beckoned to me. "Come on in," she said, "and meet the ladies."

The main meeting room, bright and spacious, was filled with women talking and laughing. They moved toward us in welcome. Tiffany introduced us to the group, then beckoned us to follow.

"The ladies wanted to show you what they've made." Lap quilts, wall quilts, and children's clothes lay on folding tables, offering a cheery welcome. All were carefully arranged and ready for us to see.

"Wow, you guys have been busy!" We admired each piece, our fingers tracing the lines of careful stitches.

We walked outside to the truck, and Kim carefully opened the back door while I turned to see a car drive up and park nearby. A smiling woman with black cropped hair stepped out.

"Hi, I'm Ginny, Deb's friend."

Deb Baer, a friend in Monona, loves bringing people together. She connected me to Reverend Walter Baer in New Orleans several years before and now had connected us to Ginny, a lifelong sewer living in Houston.

"When she's not sewing, Ginny is volunteering," Deb had said. A perfect match, Ginny was there to help. I quickly acquainted her with the machines we had in the truck, explaining their levels of complexity. The women lined up, and Ginny interviewed them one by one, asking what kind of sewing they did and their level of experience. She then turned to me with a machine recommendation. Stationed on the back ledge of the truck, I searched for the appropriate machine. Kim met me at the back of the truck to take the machine and deliver it to the new owner's car. Clipboard in hand, Ginny recorded each machine's new home. The system quickly took shape, efficient and simple.

Handing a machine to the last woman in line, I looked out across the parking lot to see Kim hugging a woman after loading her machine in the car. I saw Ginny smiling and talking with another woman, a warm hand on her shoulder. Several women talked in a group, animated and smiling. How quickly this gift had come together. Companies responded with machines, Tiffany organized recipients, a kind man with a pallet jack appeared, and a tall man materialized when we needed him. Our truck, loaded with machines, stitched its way across town, drawing a new line on the map—one invisible thread connecting everything, luminous and strong, mending one corner of a tired, water-soaked city.

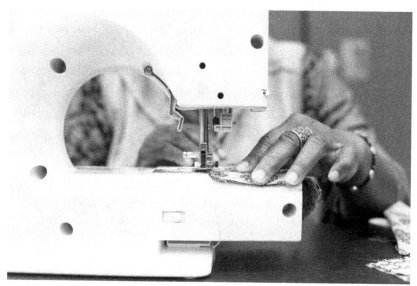

The product of sewing is just the beginning. When we come together to sew there is a sacred connection.

# Chapter 21

"Welcome!" said a woman, opening the door and introducing herself as Maria.

The rusted hinges creaked as she opened the door of the two-story house on East Johnson Street in Madison. Kim and I stepped into the cramped front hall, shaking off the cold.

"Your friend is already upstairs," Maria's hand swept the air above the narrow staircase. Small wooden steps led us to the second floor. The air, like the house, held an air of weariness with its blend of old wood, memories of past meals, and a touch of mold.

Our guide led us down the hall and pushed open the last door on the right.

"Hello!" came a cheery voice, and there was Chris, one of our board members, along with two women we'd yet to meet, a circle of chairs pulled into place for our meeting. The walls were painted church basement pink, with a few posters from past events tacked here and there. A melange of seating, I chose a rolling office chair and brought it to a proper height. Jan, a petite woman with a broad smile, introduced herself as the director of Project Respect. Teri, relaxed and easy, chimed in, "I'm Teri! I'm the one who filled out the application."

The five of us settled into comfortable conversation. Six months earlier, Teri had talked with Trish, her neighbor and our board president, about applying for sewing machines for the center. Their group, Project Respect, was on the front lines in Madison, pulling victims of sex trafficking out of the clutches of the industry. Teri had applied for ten sewing machines. We gave her fourteen to set up a sewing room in the old house, the heartbeat of Project Respect.

Trish insisted we include the extra four machines. When Trish's dear friend Kathy died after a long battle with cancer, her family gifted Kathy's four sewing machines to The Sewing Machine Project. "Kathy would love the idea of sharing these machines with Project Respect," Trish had said. "She was all about community and helping women."

Teri wasn't sure how the sewing program would go, but she knew she would set up a few machines in this makeshift space on Johnson Street. She hoped that the magnetic pull of a sewing machine would be strong enough to reach through the curtain of shame and resistance that hovered around the women who entered. In an earlier chapter of her life, Teri was a middle school home economics teacher. As home ec programs disintegrated into the air in a cloud of recipes, nutrition charts, and handmade aprons, Teri decided to reroute and became a therapist. She told her story as we gently rolled back and forth in our chairs on the well-worn floor of our meeting room.

"My two careers were the perfect combination of skills for the work I do now, though I didn't see it at the time. Becoming a therapist seemed like a natural next step, and now here I am."

Teri made the machines available during individual and group therapy sessions, letting them work their magic. Sewers understand the draw of sitting in front of a machine, with the ability to problem solve while your hands are busy creating.

"Something about sitting at the machine rather than face to face in a session," Teri said. "Or maybe having their hands busy works. A simple distraction unlocks conversation, emotion that we weren't able to access before." Teri's eyes filled with tears. "This is helping so much. Maybe it's the pride the women feel in creating something or the soft hand of the fabric." She ran her hands over the worn denim of her jeans. "For each woman, the threads weave together in a different way, but the results are similar. We see pride. We see confidence, sometimes even a glimmer of joy."

Jan spoke next. "The heaviest burden for these women is shame. Shame has a presence all its own. They are unable to see their own beauty. Living in fight-or-flight mode, losing the ability to plan forward is common. Survival depends on living in the 'right now.'"

"So, planning a sewing project is a challenge," Teri added. "As we talk about what they'll create, we reteach the ability, step by step, to think forward."

Jan nodded and smiled. "Our clients arrive here from every backdrop, connected only by threads of mistreatment and shame, but as they sew, deeper threads emerge and begin to connect them. You wouldn't imagine how two women, isolated in their trauma, can sit next to one another sewing and connect, but they do. We have one client who is all punked out and another who is so meek and quiet, but when they sew, the facades drop away. I love when I peek into a sewing session and see what's going on."

Teri looked around the room. "We are having conversations we've never had before, and sewing has opened that door. I knew this sewing room idea had potential, but this is far beyond anything I'd imagined."

Passing a box of tissues, Jan added, "There is a huge stigma connected to sex trafficking, and our clients feel shame about needing help, about needing therapy, to untangle the threads of how they got here, and how to move forward. We've had trouble in the past with clients not showing up for appointments. But not anymore."

Teri smiled. "We don't even ask if someone is coming to 'therapy' anymore. Now we say, 'Will you be in sewing class today?' And they come."

Our volunteers "keep the ship afloat"–checking machines, helping with shipments, mending, helping in the classroom. We simply would not "BE" without them.

# Chapter 22

A swath of light dances in patterns across the classroom, catching a corner of the sewing table. Two students sit opposite one another, talking quietly as they work, the light catching nimble hands. The room is awash in sound, in color, in creativity.

Since our first attempts with Bhutanese clients in 2012, our sewing classes have grown in popularity. Ten years later, the prospect of learning to sew and receiving a sewing machine has remained an attractive draw.

Like everything else The Sewing Machine Project undertakes, the decade-long process of developing these classes is always evolving. In an exercise in boundary setting, we are constantly asking, "What aligns with our mission, and what falls outside of these boundaries?" Each center is asked to create the class list, designating clients most in need of our offerings. We deliver the sewing machines, the instructor, and the volunteers. Local community organizations make annual grants to fund teachers and supplies. The center coordinates registration, available classroom space, and translators.

Class development has been an exercise in adapting. We pivot as necessary to meet the needs of each center. Pay-it-forward projects continue to evolve based on the needs of our partnering centers. Carolyn, one of our instructors, uses a tote bag project to pay it forward. The totes are handy for food pantries, senior programs, and after-school groups. We are developing a patch displaying our logo and a space for the center's and the maker's names. This way, when the bags are given away within the community, recipients will see the familiar name of one of their fellow residents on their bag.

The machines we use are beautiful. Their hum underscores the buzz of conversation, the audible hum of concentration. These matching computerized sewing machines were a gift from the Brother Corporation, a corporate champion of The Sewing Machine Project's work. Brother has been a proud supporter since 2018. These new machines supplement the well-loved machines we receive from individuals across the country. Our machines arrive in a local class, housed in brightly colored bags specifically designed for sewing machines and embroidered with the SMP logo—a gift from Bluefig, another corporate donor.

In the sewing class I'm visiting today, women carefully consider and construct tote bags, thinking about what they will carry and designing the bags to suit. A set of high-quality sewing tools allows students to snip, pin, and measure with success. The tools were a gift from a woman named Peg, a sewer in the local community. Peg reached out over a year ago, wanting to help somehow. "I want to do more than donate money," Peg said. "I'd like to donate something tangible." I thought about it and suggested that Peg put together sewing kits for our local classes. These kits convey the message that the right tool makes a difference and that the folks who receive them deserve something beautiful and new. Peg loved the idea, and together, we created a list of tools, choosing brands we've found a pleasure to use. Peg delivered them in tidy individual carrying cases, even including reading glasses. Recently, a man named Pete reached out and offered to purchase sewing kits for The SMP. Our conversation flowed as I told him about the kits Peg was creating.

"You know," I said, "it does get costly, purchasing these high-quality supplies. How about I put you in touch with Peg, and you can collaborate?" And with that, Pete ordered forty pairs of shears to include with the kits for 2023 and had them shipped to Peg. Peg gathered a group of sewing friends, and they spent a happy evening putting the kits together. Every kit carries a message of love and respect.

The mantra of offering tools that are truly a gift is embedded in The Sewing Machine Project's mission. We will not give something that feels cast off. We will not deliver something that only half works and call it a "gift." We will provide a spark of joy and hope in a weary world.

"Can I help you with that?" I turn to see a volunteer approaching a student. In addition to our instructor, we typically have two volunteers in the classroom, ready to help as needed. Barbara pulls up a chair next to the student and gently shows her how to adjust the presser foot pressure. As easily as she steps in, she steps back, allowing the student to continue on her own. The room hums. I touch base with Carolyn, the instructor, to say goodbye. Carolyn smiles as she prepares for the next lesson.

Driving across town for a drop-in at our free mending site, I am transported both within and without. Such kindness is embodied in people who hear and believe in the work of The Sewing Machine Project, whose kindness pours forth through hands and hearts.

When I arrive at the Central Library in downtown Madison, I am quickly reminded of the hub that this library is—a resource to so many. The Sewing Machine Project mending site has become one of the library's richest offerings. I hike up to the second floor to see how things are going. As expected, the menders are busy. Bird consults with a client while Ann sews.

"So, this is how I think I'll fix this," Bird says, showing the client the patch material and explaining the process. "Is this okay with you?" The older man nods.

We have two mending sites now at two Madison libraries. When COVID-19 demanded that everything close, our original three sites went quiet. Reopening a year later was an exercise in caution and careful consideration. I consulted with Bird, who suggested we reopen our most active site—at Madison Central Library, where menders work every Thursday from ten until noon. The volunteers are delighted to be back. Our second site, at Madison Hawthorne Library, opened more recently and is still being weighed and considered as we assess its popularity with both clients and volunteers. Each careful step undertaken by The SMP is an exercise in "letting it float a while" to see whether it is a good decision, whether it feels right, and whether we are truly serving in a way that is helpful. We listen, watch, and immerse ourselves, determining whether there is energy. We carefully move forward. If we don't feel energy, we back off, reassess, redirect, and see the experience as a lesson.

Our relationship with libraries is a little project unto itself. Andrew Carnegie called libraries "palaces of the people," one of the few truly free resources open to anyone. Our model fits that idea well. In addition to housing our local mending in libraries, we send many machines to libraries around the country, outfitting classes and creating tool-lending libraries. Sewing machines have even become a hands-on accompaniment to youth reading programs. The breadth and depth of sewing as a resource within libraries is a natural fit.

Many diverse groups around the United States apply for machines. Our board meets monthly to consider the applications and their alignment with our mission, and we are all reminded, again and again, of how much need exists. At the same time, we are shown the incredibly creative ways groups around the country are addressing need. Board members arrive at meetings having read, considered, and researched each applicant group. We all weigh in, and I am ever grateful for these wise women whose compassion and honesty shine. As a board, we have decided to limit our international applications. Though there is plenty of need throughout the world, we have found that vetting international groups and managing shipping logistics are tasks currently beyond us. We serve locally and nationally, asking recipient groups, when they are able, to help fund the shipping.

There are also quiet times—when winds cease, and the water is calm around the boat that is The Sewing Machine Project. In the early years, when things calmed down, I would worry. *What's going on? This can't be right! We should be moving!* Over time, I learned that the quiet times encourage us to rest, take stock, and tidy the decks. We are reminded that there is still movement in the quiet times, even when we cannot see it, and that these times are as much a part of the process as the busy times. I must remember this every time, and once I lean into the knowing, a startling sweetness occurs. When the waters are calm, my mind and heart are flooded with inspiration and a renewed tenderness for our mission. I sink into these times, swimming in new ideas and insights, my spirit rinsed fresh by the calm waters.

Once the busyness comes again, as it always does, we step into it, rested and nimble.

Bird shows the man his finished mend. "Oh, that's just fine!" he smiles, his hands moving over the familiar fabric, now with a new red patch. Having a few moments between clients, I check in to see if the menders need anything. "I think we're good!" Bird says. "These matching machines are great!" The machines were donated by a woman named Pattie in Minnesota, a retired engineer who delights in tidying up secondhand sewing machines to deliver to The Sewing Machine Project. Arriving clean, clearly labeled, and ready for delivery, these "pre-approved" machines are truly a gift. We installed two matching machines at each of our mending sites, making it easier to share presser feet, manuals, and bobbins. When I reached out to Pattie to thank her, she overflowed with excitement.

"Oh, I just love doing this, and I'm so happy to have a way to help!" Pattie's response is echoed throughout our donor community. In the face of the world's jarring realities, everyone is searching for meaning and ways to help. Financial donors find solace in helping a grassroots cause. Sewing machine donors find peace in knowing their beloved tool will see a new chapter. Volunteers look into the eyes of new sewers, excited and hopeful, and the community grows. Menders tenderly care for a beloved garment, extending its life. There is much meaning here.

I say goodbye to Bird and Ann and head back to the car. Once inside, I pause and whisper a silent thank you. Though tiny and quiet, I hope it can begin to convey the immensity of my gratitude to an unseen but unmistakable force—gratitude in the doing, gratitude in the inspiration, gratitude in the guidance, and gratitude in the love that is embodied here. Thank you.

I adjust the rearview mirror and catch a glimpse of my eyes, damp with tears, my ever-present sign that Spirit is at work, and smile. My heart is full.

"I am me."

In 2012 I drove to St. Louis and back in a day to have coffee with Frances Harrison, the BBC reporter who had written the original article that inspired the Sewing Machine Project.

# Lessons Learned

The journey of The Sewing Machine Project has been as much an evolution of an organization as an evolution of the self. I didn't set out to create a national nonprofit, but step by step, as the unfolding continued, it became clearer that this was exactly what was happening. As I learned to lead and bend with the organization, I internalized the lessons presented and found them playing out in my own life.

As I write this in 2023, I am awestruck by how far we've come, and I'm convinced we wouldn't have grown as we have without a certain degree of flexibility and, even more, grace. Here are some of the lessons that have helped me build this organization and also helped me see my own life in a whole new way:

I no longer decide that I know what the end result of something will be. While wide and creative, my own imagination is no match for the imagination of the universe. I've found that when an opportunity is presented, and I decide I know what the end will look like, I begin squishing everything into the path as I see it. Often, this hasn't ended well. So now, when an opportunity presents itself, I ask the Divine to help me see the cues I need to see, enabling me to take the steps I need to take. The unfolding is incredible, and every time, the end result is nothing I could have imagined (hint: it's always better)! The benefits along the way are really something. When we ask the Divine to guide us, our eyes are constantly open, and it's amazing how much more we see. The world becomes a much brighter place.

Creating an organization designed to serve others requires us to ask the people we hope to serve what they need. Rather than deciding people's needs based on our lived experience, we must ask the questions that will help us see the true needs. And the answers are often surprising. On a personal level, this has helped me take a breath before I forge ahead doing something I imagine someone needs and instead taking a good hard look and listening to the situation to realize what would truly be a gift.

There have been many quiet times in the unfolding of The Sewing Machine Project—times when there may be fewer requests for machines, when donation levels are lower than usual, and when the gifts we hoped to receive to do our work just aren't there. My first reaction is to think something is wrong. *Oh no, the organization is tanking!* Time and time again, I'm reminded that it's simply a wintering time. I've learned I need to trust that the seeds of our work are lying quietly under the earth, busy in their dormancy. I need to listen and respond to the resulting quiet as a time we are called to rest in preparation for the next busy phase. As a person who is often on the go, I find it hard to rest, to receive these periods of quiet grace when we are given a chance to recover. As we live into this truth, we always find that rest is necessary for the next busy time. We cannot expect to listen and compassionately respond if we do not give our bodies the rest they need.

I've learned the importance of aligning feet with words. If we say one thing is important and foundational to us, but our actions speak differently, then our words are meaningless.

*Failure* is a tricky word. Just because something doesn't turn out as planned, I am quite sure it doesn't mean it is a failure. I've learned to listen to what each experience has to teach. As long as we can extract a lesson, there is no failure.

"Listen to the sounds of inspiration inside yourself—those ideas that simmer just below the surface. I'm talking about that voice that guides you to put your goodness into the world. Listen to that voice and then follow for just a few steps. Follow and see what happens. You do not need to know where you are going—just begin. You may find that the path keeps growing longer and wider as you carefully take each step. And as you take each step, you can do the next little thing to help make the world a little better. No matter two or ten steps, you will make the world a better place as you go. Our world is aching for wholehearted efforts to help and heal. The world needs your good ideas."

-MARGARET JANKOWSKI

# Author Bio

MARGARET JOHN JANKOWSKI is a writer, maker, and nonprofit leader living in Madison, Wisconsin. She is the founder and director of The Sewing Machine Project. A lifelong sewist, Margaret's mind is "on fire" when she is planning a project in three dimensions. The Sewing Machine Project represents the intersection of Margaret's passions as it provides the opportunity to sew, serve, and write about the incredible individuals she encounters.

Margaret divides her time between her home in Wisconsin and Switzerland, where she spends time with her husband, Peter. Margaret finds deep joy in traveling, reading, walking with friends, and sitting and laughing on the front porch with her two kids.

# Acknowledgments

"If the only prayer you ever say in your
entire life is thank you, it will be enough."

-MEISTER ECKHART

My heart is filled with thank yous. The chorus of voices that have risen with the growth of The Sewing Machine Project fills me and ignites me. So many have voiced their support, and this belief in the power of an idea has truly kept my flame alive.

Many have shared financial gifts which have formed and strengthened the structural foundation of The Sewing Machine Project. I am so grateful for your belief in me and the mission of The SMP.

Many board members have offered so much wisdom over the years. Your deep commitment and guidance have been integral to the growth of the organization.

Our volunteers form the backbone of The Sewing Machine Project. I thank these generous souls for their incredible passion and time they pour into our initiatives. Seeing the way each of you pours love into The SMP is truly a thing of beauty.

We hear from groups all over the country who are recognizing and addressing need in such creative ways. You inspire me and keep hope alive for all the good in the world.

To everyone who has received a sewing machine from The Sewing Machine Project and found hope in this creative tool, thank you for your inspiration. Your story matters.

Writing is a solitary act, but producing a book takes a team. So many have cheered me on, read and reread drafts of this book, and offered their encouragement and suggestions. I am so grateful. Julie Tallard Johnson, Jan Christian, and Michelle Wildgen, you read my early drafts and kindly offered content editing and constructive criticism. Marianne Fons, you appeared just when I needed you, thoroughly and gently copyediting my manuscript. Carl, my long-time friend, you created such beautiful cover art. Many thanks to the Little Creek Press team for inviting me into the process and for accompanying me every step of the way.

We, together, bring this book to the fore.

And to my dearest home team—

Peter, you offer honest insights, unwavering support, and love. I am so grateful to have you by my side.

Mom, you've been interested and supportive every step of the way, and you even had wardrobe suggestions when needed.

Alec and Maddie, you are the smartest, funniest people on the planet. Thank you for believing in and supporting your mom's idea. I love you beyond anything I've ever known.

To learn more about The Sewing Machine Project, please visit our website: TheSewingMachineProject.org

# Book Club Questions

1. Margaret writes that "the idea landed like a whisper" after she read a BBC news report about a Sri Lankan woman named Vahashani, who hoped that her sewing machine had survived the horrific 2004 tsunami. "With my 'yes,' a door swung open." Have you ever said "yes" to something that changed your life's course?

2. A sewing machine seems a humble object, but it symbolized women's empowerment in cultures ranging from Kosovo to Sri Lanka to right here in Madison, where women who had been trafficked for sex learned to sew as part of their healing. What is it about sewing that is so powerful?

3. Many of the donated sewing machines came with hand-written notes about their owners and histories. If your sewing machine could talk, what story would it tell?

4. Margaret describes being guided, reassured by dreams. Have you ever had a dream that helped you solve a problem? Guided you? Describe it.

5. Just as a talented seamstress can turn an old garment into something new, the Sewing Machine Project pushed Margaret from her introvert self into someone who appears on television, gives speeches to thousands and travels the world with near strangers. Can you recall a time in your life when something pushed you out of your comfort zone?

6. The Sewing Machine Project brought all kinds of people into Margaret's life: Mardi Gras Indians Big Chief Howard Miller and Queen Rukiya Brown, the regulars at the Mother-in-Law Lounge, the quilters of Gee's Bend, Nancy Zieman of Sewing with Nancy, Cherice Harrison Nelson, the ladies of Kosovo, and the homeless people here in Madison who wait patiently while their belongings are tended to by the menders at the library. Does a particular character stand out to you?

7. The people in New Orleans pledged to "pay it forward" by doing mending for neighbors, making baby blankets for the hospital and teaching others to sew. What are other ways sewers can pay it forward?

8. Not everything worked the way Margaret envisioned it. The SeaHope bags, sewn of old sails to benefit the Houma community in Louisiana, had problems from the start. What lessons were learned from that project?

9. The mending project also seems to create community and a chance to help people who sometimes have very few possessions. Can you think of other services needed in your community?

10. Margaret writes, "The imagination of the universe is far greater than my own." Describe a time when you experienced a challenge and the answer was a complete surprise.

Printed in the USA
CPSIA information can be obtained
at www.ICGtesting.com
LVHW071936140923
758215LV00007B/176